George A. Henderson

Early Saint John Methodism

and history of Centenary Methodist Church, Saint John, N.B. - a jubilee souvenir

George A. Henderson

Early Saint John Methodism
and history of Centenary Methodist Church, Saint John, N.B. - a jubilee souvenir

ISBN/EAN: 9783337260149

Printed in Europe, USA, Canada, Australia, Japan

Cover: Foto ©Lupo / pixelio.de

More available books at **www.hansebooks.com**

EARLY SAINT JOHN METHODISM

AND

HISTORY

OF

Centenary Methodist Church

SAINT JOHN, N. B.

A Jubilee Souvenir.

EDITED BY

GEO. A. HENDERSON.

"*Tell ye your children of it, and let your children tell their children, and their children another generation.*"—JOEL.

SAINT JOHN, N. B.:
PRESS OF GEO. E. DAY, GERMAIN STREET.
1890.

PREFACE.

CENTENARY CHURCH having completed its fiftieth year, a committee was appointed by the Trustee and Quarterly Boards to prepare a programme, the carrying out of which would give due recognition to that event. The duty of preparing a paper, in which leading facts connected with the church's history should be noted, was assigned to me, coupled with the further duty of reading the same at some time during the celebration. It was soon found, however, that no matter how concisely the statements might be made, if the paper was to be at all complete, too much time would be demanded for its presentation. I was then asked to prepare an historical sketch, something in the nature of what is presented in the following pages, which, with an account of the Jubilee itself, should be published in book form as a Jubilee Souvenir. The duty having been accepted, was found to be much more arduous than anticipated. A paper, incomplete in itself, was prepared and read at one of the exercises during the Jubilee season, but further than that, in consequence of pressure of business, no attention could possibly be given to the subject for some months. After many days, I now present the result of my search, conscious of imperfection, and with no claim to literary merit, yet with a satisfaction that in a few instances I have rescued some items that soon might have been among the things forgotten.

There are many incidents in the history of a church which, for the time being, demand little attention. Years afterwards they are brought to the surface and yield an interest which it was not thought attached to them. With the itinerant system, of necessity there are many changes in the pastorate; moreover, the congregation is constantly changing. As a rule, no record is kept beyond matters of routine. It is a difficulty involving some research to ascertain the consecutive appointments to a Methodist circuit for any considerable number of years. Few members of Centenary could supply the information, or with accuracy detail events connected with its history. If there is any importance in the preservation of these events, as to which there ought to be little doubt, it would seem that an annual record should be prepared, to be at intervals consolidated.

It has been the aim in the preparation of the following pages to bring together items which the compiler trusts may be of interest to the congregation —items which hitherto have had but a fragmentary existence, in some instances culled from books, newspapers, or old letters, in others found chiseled on tombstones, while others again are the result of personal interviews with men and women identified with the church since its opening. Perhaps undue prominence has been given to some names and incidents, while others have not received that recognition that their virtue and importance merited. This should be accounted for by the fact that the duty at all was undertaken by one whose personal knowledge of the men and things of which he has written was very limited. Of the difficulties encountered it is not necessary to make mention. The suggestion comes that had the work been undertaken before the 20th June, 1877, the result could have been more satisfactory. Records, documents and valuable data containing information of great interest to him who would search for history were by the great fire of that day reduced to ashes and forever lost. The question may be asked, Why go back of 1839? The answer is that Centenary Church did not begin with that date. A church is not the building in which the people meet, but it is the company of believers who assemble within its walls. In the year 1839 the Chapel, as it was then called, on what was known as Great George street, opened its doors to the necessities of the time, and the congregation of the old church divided, part going out from and part remaining within the walls in which, for thirty years, the people called Methodists had worshipped, and even as before that date, so afterwards, down to the year 1867, by reason of an intermingling of interests and joint management of affairs, in a great measure the history of one is the history of the other.

In the preparation of this record I desire to acknowledge the help received from the invaluable history of "Methodism in Eastern British America," by Rev. T. Watson Smith. His work should be in every Methodist home. With the exception of what has been taken from Marsden's Narrative, Richey's Memoir of Rev. William Black, and "Humbert's Recollections," the early pages have been largely compiled from Mr. Smith's history. To that gentleman I am also indebted for many dates, circuit appointments, and other information of value. I desire also to acknowledge the help extended by Jos. W. Lawrence, Esq., whose interest in matters of this kind is manifest, and whose aid is always cheerfully given. The cut of "Old Germain Street Church" was loaned by him. To Dr. Withrow I am indebted for the cuts of Dr. Wood and "Centenary as it was." To Dr. McLeod, of Baltimore; Peter LeSueur, of Ottawa, one of the early officials of Centenary; Rev. H. Daniel, James Sullivan and R. W. Thorne, for their recollections; and to E. T. C. Knowles, for the Sunday School and Love Feast report, I thankfully acknowledge the assistance rendered.

The time spent in the preparation of these pages has been cheerfully given. My reward is a stronger attachment to my church. The work now finished was undertaken as a duty, and is, with its deficiencies, passed over to the congregation, who look upon the church somewhat with the feelings of him who wrote of Giotto's tower:

"Blossoming in stone,
A vision, a delight, and a desire,
The builder's perfect and centennial flower,
That in the night of ages bloomed alone,
But wanting still the glory of the spire."

G. A. H.

MINISTERS STATIONED AT ST. JOHN PRIOR TO OPENING OF CENTENARY CHURCH.

1791—ABRAHAM J. BISHOP.
1794—WILLIAM JESSOP.
1795—DANIEL FIDLER.
* 1801—JAMES MANN, THOMAS OLIVANT.
1802—JOSHUA MARSDEN.
1803—WILLIAM BENNETT.
1804—JOSHUA MARSDEN.
1808—WILLIAM BENNETT.
1809—WILLIAM BLACK.
1811—STEPHEN BAMFORD.
1813—JAMES KNOWLAN.
1815—WILLIAM CROSCOMBE.
1817—STEPHEN BAMFORD.
1819—JAMES PRIESTLY.
1821—ROBERT ALDER.
1823—JAMES PRIESTLY.
1824—ROBERT ALDER.
1826—RICHARD WILLIAMS.
1828—RICHARD WILLIAMS, ENOCH WOOD.
1829 JOHN BASS STRONG, ENOCH WOOD.
1830—JOHN B. STRONG, ALBERT DESBRISAY.
1831—ALBERT DESBRISAY, J. B. STRONG, SAMUEL JOLL.
1832—ALBERT DESBRISAY, SAMUEL JOLL.
1833—SAMPSON BUSBY, WILLIAM SMITHSON.
1835—SAMPSON BUSBY, ARTHUR McNUTT.
1836—ENOCH WOOD, ARTHUR McNUTT.
1837 ENOCH WOOD, RICHARD SHEPHARD.

* In other years the circuit, which covered a great part of the province, was visited by two or three ministers in the course of a year. The list of these comprised Duncan McColl, James Mann, William Earley, James Boyd and William Grandin.

MINISTERS TO ST. JOHN SOUTH CIRCUIT.

1839—RICHARD WILLIAMS, *FREDERICK SMALLWOOD.
1840—WILLIAM TEMPLE, *F. SMALLWOOD.
1841—WM. TEMPLE, *S. D. RICE, HUMPHREY PICKARD.
1842—WM. TEMPLE, *ENOCH WOOD, WM. ALLEN.
1843—*ENOCH WOOD, GEORGE MILLER, DAVID JENNINGS.
1844—*ENOCH WOOD, GEORGE MILLER.
1845—*ENOCH WOOD, GEORGE MILLER, F. SMALLWOOD.
1846—HENRY DANIEL, *INGHAM SUTCLIFFE.
1849—RICHARD KNIGHT, *ROBERT COONEY.
1852—RICHARD KNIGHT, *JOHN ALLISON.
1853—JAMES G. HENNIGAR, *WM. T. CARDY.
1854—JAS. G. HENNIGAR, *W. T. CARDY, GEO. B. PAYSON.
1855—JAS. G. HENNIGAR, *W. T. CARDY, CHAS. STEWART.
1856—E. BOTTERILL, *T. M. ALBRIGHTON, C. STEWART.
1858—E. BOTTERILL, *WM. WILSON, T. M. ALBRIGHTON.
1859—J. MCMURRAY, *WM. WILSON, JOHN LATHERN.
1860—J. MCMURRAY, *WM. WILSON, J. R. NARRAWAY.
1861—J. MCMURRAY, *M. RICHEY, D. D., JOHN LATHERN.
1862—M. RICHEY, D. D., *J. R. NARRAWAY, A. W. NICHOLSON
1864—JOHN S. ADDY, *J. R. NARRAWAY, JOHN BREWSTER.
1865—JOHN S. ADDY, *J. R. NARRAWAY, J. L. SPONAGLE.
1866—JOHN S. ADDY, *JAMES ENGLAND, J. L. SPONAGLE.

MINISTERS TO CENTENARY CIRCUIT.

1867—JAMES ENGLAND.
1868—JOHN LATHERN.
1871—DUNCAN D. CURRIE.
1873—HENRY POPE.
1876—HOWARD SPRAGUE.
1878—HOWARD SPRAGUE, MATTHEW R. KNIGHT.
1879—JOSEPH HART.
1880—D. D. CURRIE.
1883—WILLIAM DOBSON.
1886—WALDRON W. BREWER.
1889—EDWIN EVANS.

*These had the pastoral oversight of the Centenary congregation.

CENTENARY METHODIST CHURCH.

PASTOR: REV. EDWIN EVANS.
Residence, - - - - - *277 Princess Street.*

SERVICES.

Sunday—11 a. m., 7 p. m.
Sabbath School— 2.30 p. m.; Superintendent, J. McA. Hutchings; Assistant Superintendent, J. L. Thorne.
Bible Class for Gentlemen—Conducted by James Sullivan.
Young Mens' Bible Class—Conducted by J. E. Irvine.
Young Ladies' Bible Classes—Conducted by Mrs. Hea and Miss Mary B. Smith.
Infant Class—Conducted by Mrs. E. B. McLaughlin and Miss L. McLaughlin.

WEEK-NIGHT MEETINGS.

Wednesday, 8 p. m.—Preaching Service.
Friday, 8 p. m.—Prayer Meeting.

SOCIETY CLASSES.

Sunday—10 a. m., Joseph Prichard, James Sullivan, J. E. Irvine, H. J. Thorne, R. M. Smith, Miss Fannie E. Henderson.
Tuesday—3 p. m., Joseph Prichard; 4 p. m., Mrs. Hea.
Wednesday—3 p. m., Mrs. Eaton.
Thursday—4 p. m., Mrs. Hea; 4 p. m., Miss Sarah E. Smith.
Friday—3 p. m., the Minister; 4 p. m., Mrs. McLaughlin.

MEMBERS OF QUARTERLY OFFICIAL BOARD.

Ministers—Rev. Edwin Evans (chairman), Rev. H. Daniel, Rev. J. R. Narraway, Rev. Henry Pope, D D.
Local Preachers and Exhorters—James Sullivan, E. T. C. Knowles, Fred. S. Skinner, Thomas Cassidy, J. E. Irvine, H. J. Thorne.
Stewards—Caleb W. Wetmore, J. Lefferts Thorne, Richard W. McCarty, Joshua S. Turner, I. C. Bowman, John Sealy, Joshua Clawson, Recording Steward.
Class Leaders—James Sullivan, Joseph Prichard, J. McA. Hutchings, J. E. Irvine, H. J. Thorne, R. M. Smith, Mrs. Hea, Mrs. E. B. McLaughlin, Miss S. E. Smith, Mrs. Julia Eaton, Miss F. E. Henderson.
Representatives of the Society—G. A. Henderson, W. G. Smith, Geo. Jenkins, Charles D. Stewart, R. W. Thorne, John Sealy, Wm. Greig.
Superintendent of Sunday School—J. McA. Hutchings.

CENTENARY METHODIST CHURCH.

TRUSTEES CENTENARY CHURCH.

R. W. Thorne.	Gilbert Bent.	Joseph Prichard.
D. J. McLaughlin, Jr.	C. W. Wetmore.	Henry J. Thorne.
A. A. Stockton.	Hiram B. White.	Edwin Frost.
L. H. Vaughan.	John E. Irvine.	W. H. Hayward.
Thomas A. Temple.	Judge Palmer.	G. A. Henderson.
J. McA. Hutchings.	Wm. C. Godsoe.	E. T. C. Knowles.

G. A. Henderson, Trustee Steward.

SABBATH SCHOOL.

Sessions held each Sabbath at 2:30 p. m.

COMMITTEE OF MANAGEMENT.

Officers of School.
- J. McA. Hutchings, Superintendent.
- J. L. Thorne, Assistant Superintendent.
- W. C. Jordan, Secretary.
- W. G. Smith, Treasurer.
- Charles D. Stewart, Librarian.
- M. G. B. Henderson, Assistant Librarian.
- R. M. McLaughlin,   "   "
- Sidney Dinsmore,   "   "
- R. Morton Smith, Musical Director.
- Miss Jennie McLaughlin, Organist.
- Miss Mitchell, Assistant Organist.
- W. Morley P. McLaughlin, Organist to Infant Class.

Teachers.
- J. E. Irvine,
- James Sullivan,
- H. J. Thorne,
- J. Clawson.
- G. A. Henderson.
- W. G. Smith,
- George Jenkins,
- R. M. Smith,
- E. T. C. Knowles,
- J. H. White,
- Thomas Jenkins,
- John Sealy.
- Mrs. C. E. Macmichael,
- Miss Maggie Sharp,
- " Fannie E. Henderson,
- Mrs. Hea,
- Miss M. B. Smith,
- Miss Palmer,
- Mrs. E. T. C. Knowles,
- Miss A. Emma Whittaker,
- " Mary V. Henderson,
- " Sarah E. Smith,
- " McKillop,
- Mrs. G. A. Henderson,
- Miss Maud Narraway,
- " Minnie Godsoe,
- " Kate Turner,
- " Mary Whittaker,
- " Lilly Whittaker,
- " Hattie P. Thorne,

Mrs. E. B. McLaughlin, Infant Class.
Miss Laura McLaughlin, Asst.   do.

Representatives appointed by Quarterly Board—Jos. Prichard, R. W. Thorne, R. W. McCarty, J. S. Turner, C. W. Wetmore.

Miss F. E. Palmer, Treasurer Missionary Committee.
Miss Mary B. Smith, Supt. of Band of Mercy.

SOCIETIES.

Woman's Missionary Society—Mrs. C. E. Macmichael, President;. Miss A. Emma Whittaker, Recording Secretary; Miss Sarah E. Barrett, Corresponding Secretary; Miss Mary U. Henderson, Treasurer.

Mite Society—Miss Kate R. Bartlett, President; Miss Fannie E. Palmer, Treasurer.

Haraiwa Band—Miss Bartlett, President; Miss Laura McLaughlin, Secretary.

Sustentation Aid Society, \
Dorcas Society, } Composed of ladies of several Methodist Churches. \
King's Daughters,

CHURCH COMMITTEES.

Missionary Committee—Geo. A. Henderson, E. T. C. Knowles, J. McA. Hutchings, H. J. Thorne, J. Clawson, J. E. Irvine, C. D. Stewart.

Joint Finance Committee—Judge Palmer, A. A. Stockton, G. A. Henderson, Trustees; J. S. Turner, —— ——, J. Clawson, Quarterly Board.

Committee to Promote the Circulation of the "Wesleyan"—John E. Irvine, G. A. Henderson, H. J. Thorne, E. T. C. Knowles.

Musical Committee—Howard D. Troop, Joseph Allison, Henry J. Thorne, J. W. Daniel, M. D., Joshua Clawson.

Parsonage Furnishing Committee—Mrs. Prichard, Mrs. J. V. Troop, Mrs. R. W. Thorne, Mrs. E. T. Knowles, Mrs. H. J. Thorne, Mrs. Irvine, Mrs. G. A. Henderson, Mrs. J. E. Whittaker, Mrs. W. H. Hayward, Mrs. Philip Palmer, Mrs. S. J. King, Mrs. Tuck.

ERRATA.

Page 13, 5th line—For "antinomain" read "antinomian."
" 18, 23rd line—For "itineracy" read "itinerancy."
" 90, 19th line—For "6th" read "3rd."
" 122, 1st line—For "16th" read "18th."

Early Saint John Methodism

AND

HISTORY OF CENTENARY CHURCH.

TO everything there is a beginning; but sometimes the origin of what has developed into a great work may be involved in obscurity.

The date of the organization of Methodism in Saint John is not a matter of conjecture, but, by reason of the thoughtfulness of those connected with it, is so well authenticated that there can be no dispute about its inception.

Among the Loyalists who, on the 18th day of May, 1783, landed on the rugged shore,—where now is the Market Slip of the city of Saint John,—was a New Jersey Methodist, whose name was Stephen Humbert. From his arrival, and throughout a long and honorable life, he was a moving spirit in the city of the Loyalists. He was a captain in the militia; an alderman of the city; and became a representative in the House of Assembly. At a period, when Methodism was somewhat under social ban, he did not shrink from using in a legitimate way the influence which his official position gave him for the advancement of the interests of the church of his choice.

The first residents of Saint John were chiefly adherents of the Church of England. Through the solicitations of Mr. Humbert and a few others who had been accustomed to other forms of worship than those of the dominant church, several ministers, among whom was Henry Alline, visited the growing town, held services, tarried a brief period, and went on their way. The country was not yet opened; travelling was beset with difficulties; the journeys undertaken were both tedious and uncomfortable, and, as a consequence, except in the larger communities, the bread of life was seldom broken.

The devoted band mentioned above, not more loyal to their king than to their faith, yearning for the spiritual teaching that harmonized with their views, made application to influential Methodists in New York to the end that a preacher might be appointed to Saint John. In this they were successful, and so fortunate as to secure the appointment of Abraham John Bishop. Mr. Bishop had been possessed of wealth, had good prospects of worldly success, but was so convinced of his call to the ministry that he accepted the commission; gave up business prospects, and devoted all his property to the work of God, making provision that one-half should go to missions and the balance should be applied to the promotion of the interests of Methodism in the Channel Islands,—a part of the funds set apart for the latter purpose are still held in the hands of the trustees in accordance with the donor's wish. He became a candidate for the Methodist ministry; was appointed to New Brunswick. Sailed from the Downs on the 18th July; reached Halifax 30th August, and Saint John on the 24th September, 1791. In appearance he is said to have been very attractive; his bearing always that of a Christian and a gentleman, a sweet serenity adorned a countenance on which a smile was seldom seen, but every feature of which indicated a mind influenced to purposes of a noble order. He was in the noblest sense of the word, a man of God, and possessed a large share of the genuine missionary spirit. Wise, prudent, loving, he feared neither small nor great, but would lovingly invite or mildly reprove all with whom he had any intercourse. He rarely met an individual on the streets without speaking to him, if an occasion afforded, on the great concerns of his soul and eternity. Such were his character and zeal.

On the first Sunday after his arrival he preached from I. John, i., 3: "That which we have seen and heard declare we unto you, that ye also may have fellowship with us; and truly our fellowship is with the Father and with his Son Jesus Christ." On the first Sabbath in October he organized a class meeting in a house owned by John Kelly, situate on lot 625, being the southeast corner of Princess and Charlotte streets. Cynthia Kelly, wife of the owner of the house, was appointed leader of the class.* This, then, was the beginning of Methodism in Saint John.

Mr. Bishop had letters of introduction from Governor Parr, of Nova Scotia, and Philip Marchinton, of Halifax, to the Mayor of the city of Saint John, which were of the value of a license, and, no doubt, saved him from much trouble.

The population was small and the community was not pre-

---

*On Sunday last, 6th September, 1829, after a long and painful illness, Mrs. Cynthia Kelly, relict of the late Mr. John Kelly, carpenter. Mrs. K. has been an acceptable member of the Wesleyan Methodist Society from the introduction of Methodism in this city, to the time of her decease,- a period of nearly forty years. And, as during the whole of that time, her chief object and aim was to adorn her religious profession by a corresponding life and conversation; so under her protracted illness she was divinely supported and comforted, and her death was peaceful and happy.—*Religious and Literary Journal, 12th September, 1829.*

pared to accept as an element in its life the zeal of the people called Methodists, and an intolerant spirit was manifested to such a degree as to resist which required much tact and courage. Soon after the arrival of this Methodist preacher, the Mayor was informed that he was not only preaching on Sabbath evening, but on week evenings also, and that some, through attendance on his ministry, were becoming crazy. At that time Episcopal services were held on Sabbath mornings only. A few days after the report had reached the Mayor's ears, Mr. Bishop met him, with some of the aldermen, a military officer and several other gentlemen on the Market Square, and stopped to pay his respects to them. "I am sorry," said the Mayor, "to hear some strange accounts of your preaching. I hear that you not only preach on Sundays, but on week evenings also, and that some of your hearers are going beside themselves. Can't you be content to preach on Sundays, as other clergymen do?" Mr. Bishop, in reply, assured the Mayor that he had not heard of any of the members of his congregation having become insane through his preaching, and promised him that, if informed of any, he would do his best to bring them to their senses. At the same time, he avowed his sincere belief that the gospel which he preached was likely to have the contrary effect in making those who listened to it wise unto salvation. He did not change his course in consequence of this interview, but as a writer has said, "His spirit glowed with holy zeal. No victor gloried more in trophies won by his sword than did Bishop over those in whom he saw the happy results of the travail of his Redeemer's soul." So far from confining himself to a single service on the Sabbath, as the Mayor had suggested, house to house prayer meetings, led by himself, were held, whenever possible, in dwellings crowded to the very street, and bore witness to the untiring zeal of the minister.

The first framed house finished by the Loyalists was a place of worship. This building stood on the east side of Germain Street, between Duke and Queen streets, on lot No. 121, now owned by Mr. John McMillan, and was thirty-six by twenty-eight feet. It was purchased for £140, and at an additional cost of £90 was fitted for church purposes. Besides being used as the church it was known as the Court House and City Hall. Here were the gatherings of church and state. In this building the early city fathers held their meetings, presided over by Gabriel G. Ludlow. Here, also, the first judges of New Brunswick, George D. Ludlow, James Putnam, Isaac Allen and Joshua Upham, administered law; here George Bisset, the first Episcopal rector, ministered, as well as Mather Byles, who succeeded him. Here, also, the first confirmation in New Brunswick was held, and Bishop Inglis, first bishop of British North America, delivered his charge to the Episcopal clergy in 1789. In this interesting building the Episcopalians worshipped until old Trinity was opened on Christmas day, 1791. As the Episcopalians left the building the Methodists entered into possession of it on the same Christmas day, paying therefor the sum of £200, as indicated by a resolution passed at a vestry meeting 8th December, 1791, which is as follows: *Resolved*, That the old church be sold; price £200. The bell, organ and king's coat of arms be removed to Trinity church.

On the 1st of April, 1792, Mr. Bishop wrote: "The society in Saint John are increased to eighty, above half of whom have found peace with God. They have purchased a church ready furnished with pulpits and galleries, and the people continue to attend diligently. The experience of the young converts is truly wonderful,—children of ten, twelve and fifteen years of age rejoice in a pardoning God; and some persons of about sixty years of age are snatched from the pit of destruction."

Prior to this date Mr. Black, who was stationed at Halifax,

visited Saint John, while Mr. Bishop went up the river. To use his own expression, his time was "all taken up between the mount and the multitude." From Richey's memoir of Black, we find that in his efforts to benefit the multitude he experienced an unexpected interruption, the nature and cause of which were as follows: Walking the street on the Lord's day he saw certain shipbuilders and caulkers pursuing their ordinary employments. Against this public desecration of the Sabbath he felt it his duty to bear his testimony in terms of merited reprobation in his discourse in the evening. Exasperated by the exposure of their guilt, some of the individuals implicated, aware of the existence of a provincial statute against any one exercising ministerial functions without a license from the Governor, and having ascertained that the preacher had not used the precaution to procure such a license, thought it would be a worthy method of expressing their resentment, if possible, to seal the lips which had testified of them that their deeds were evil. Accordingly they preferred a charge of contempt of the law against him to the Clerk of the Peace, whose zeal in promoting their views must be admitted to have been a little more ardent than fidelity to his official responsibilities really demanded. He immediately sent a note to Mr. Black, of which the following is a copy:

To Rev. Mr. Black.

Sir: You are, I doubt not, acquainted with an act of the General Assembly of this province which inflicts a penalty upon any person who shall presume to preach, etc., without a license for that purpose, under the hand and seal of the Governor, or Commander-in-Chief for the time being. As Clerk of the Peace for this city, I conceive it my duty to enquire whether you are in possession of any such license.

I am, etc.,

E. HARDY, Clerk of the Peace.

Three hours after the above was handed to Mr. Black, he

waited on the writer at his office, and stated to him that immediately on his arrival in this Province he had consulted two of the principal magistrates of the city respecting the law in question, who assured him that it never was designed to prevent any minister regularly ordained and of sober character from communicating religious knowledge; and that in their estimation it would be quite sufficient for him to transmit the credentials of his ordination to the Governor, who, they made no doubt, would give him a license. In comformity with this suggestion, he further informed the Clerk of the Peace, that he had forwarded to His Excellency a copy of his ordination credentials, signed by Judges Ludlow and Upham, the latter of whom accompanied them with his recommendation, and at the same time remarked to him (Mr. Black), that as it was at the desire of a respectable body of people he preached, no one could look upon his compliance, under all the circumstances, as indicating a contempt of the Provincial Legislature; adding that the Governor had to his knowledge, in a similar case, referred to the magistrates, and that the professed object of the act was to *secure*, not *abridge*, liberty of conscience, or the sacred right of all persons to worship God according to the dictates of their judgment. From these considerations, said Mr. Black, I have ventured to preach at the request of the people, and intended to do so until I should hear from the Governor; but since my conduct has been construed into contempt of authority, I shall desist until I hear from the Rev. Mr. Bishop, who has gone to wait upon His Excellency. To all this Mr. Hardy replied, with considerable warmth, that neither the magistrates nor the Governor himself had any right to dispense with the law; expressed his surprise at such observations, and throwing the statute before Mr. Black, said, "You may examine it for yourself," and abruptly left the office. The opponents of Methodism, or rather of the gospel, thus gained a malignant triumph, and, emboldened by success, became loud in their boastings and predicted that the benevolent object of their hate would speedily be looking through the grates of the prison. But none of these things moved him. Interdicted from holding forth the word of life *publicly*, he endeavored, as far as practicable, to accomplish the objects of his mission by pastoral visitation, as well as preaching *from house to house*. More than a fortnight elapsed, and no license or information from the seat of government arrived,—most likely because Mr. Bishop did not happen to find His Excellency at home. Mr. Black then returned to Halifax.

Mr. Bishop continued his labors and was the instrument of the growth of evangelical religion, not only in the city of Saint John, but along the river and as far as Fredericton. In the early spring of 1792, Mr. Black again visited Saint John, but under circumstances more agreeable than those under which he had left it the preceding December. Mr. Bishop's labors had been greatly blessed. There were about seventy in the society, and the work was still progressive. In April, Mr. Bishop wrote : " I need help, for my body is very weak, and the work is great, both here and up the river. I hope the conference will send us men filled with faith and the fruit thereof." Mr. Black in the meantime had visited Fredericton, Sheffield and other points on the river, and also Saint Stephen, from which place he returned to Saint John in May. Mr. Bishop's time in the city was now expired, and on the evening of May 16th, he preached his last sermon in the city. His text was : " Finally, brethren, farewell. Be perfect, be of good comfort, be of one mind, live in peace ; and the God of love and peace shall be with you." Mr. Black, in his journal, says : " I then gave a discourse on the Lord's supper, and administered the ordinance, after which Brother McColl gave an exhortation. Singing, prayer, and exhortation followed the communion service, and when the midnight hour drew near the congregation dispersed." Continuing from Mr.

Black's journal: "Going round among the people the next day, I found them deeply distressed at the thought of losing dear Mr. Bishop, whose memory they have, indeed, cause to love." In the morning he, whom they loved, went on board the vessel and was borne out of their sight. He went to Cumberland, and in September left for Baltimore, from thence he was sent to Grenada, where one who could preach in both French and English was required. Dr. Coke introduced him to the society in January, and on the 16th June, 1793, he died of yellow fever. In the course of a sermon preached on the Sabbath of his last week on earth, he said, "I have shown you how to live. I will now show you how to die." In the Minutes of Conference for 1794, his brethren say of him, "He was one of the holiest young men on earth. He lived continually within the veil, and his soul uninterruptedly burned for the salvation of souls. He was instant in season and out of season; a useful preacher all the day long, without the least breach of modesty and decorum."

Mr. Bishop was succeeded in appointment by William Jessop, though some others in the year 1793 visited the city for short periods. He labored in Saint John one year, and did not escape the opposition to which Mr. Black was subjected,—complaint was made against him in like manner for preaching without license. The Clerk of the Peace accorded him different treatment than that which Mr. Black had received, giving him the assurance that he would not be prosecuted if he but made application for license. That being done he was allowed to minister even without having taken the oath of allegiance. Mr. Smith says of him, "He was one of the noblest of our pioneers." In Saint John large congregations, attracted by his style of preaching and his pleasant voice, listened to the pastor; but it seemed to him that his failing strength was being spent for naught. Early in the spring he resolved to leave the city and proceed to Westmorland, where he thought he would be more useful. He soon returned to the United States, and in December, 1795, at Strasbury, Penr., he died, exclaiming, "My work is done! Glory! Glory!" Bishop Asbury preached his funeral sermon. At the close of the service Asbury wrote in his journal: "I had my difficulties in speaking of a man so well known, and so much beloved. He was always solemn, and few such holy, steady men have we found among us." Jesse Lee, the founder of Methodism in New England, who greatly loved him, wept over his grave, when five years later he visited it. A note, written by the hand of a friend, and signed by Jessop himself a few days before death, conveys a request to one of his executors, illustrative of the simplicity and poverty of the ministry of that day: "I will," it was written, "that my wearing apparel be carried to the General Conference at Baltimore next; and that the same be distributed among the preachers that stand most in need of it." This appendix to his will was prompted, it is probable, by the recollection that to his brethren he was indebted for the outfit, which a stern father had denied him at the commencement of his ministry.

At the conference held in Windsor, in 1795, the only appointments to New Brunswick were those of Daniel Fidler and Duncan McColl,—the former having the city of Saint John and the appointments on the river as far up as there were any, and the latter having Saint Stephen and the region round about. Mr. Fidler previous to this, in his journey through the woods to the Scotch settlement on the Nashwaak, had for his guide Alexander McLeod, a son of one of the Highland settlers there. A son of Mr. Fidler, now living in Philadelphia, has in his possession a number of most interesting letters addressed to his father, and having kindly placed them at the disposal of the writer, the following extracts are made from them. Mr. Jessop, in a letter dated January 15th, 1795, from Saint John, says: "I am still riding in a heavy gale, by the anchor of Hope; the cloud is not yet broken, nor the storm over. What will become of this people I know not, but hope they will, after my departure, get some good, loving servant of God that shall be made a greater blessing to them than I have been. As touching my own state, I am still going on in my old way, observing the same rule and minding the same thing, in which I hope to move until I shall move no more. My dear Daniel, live near to God. Be thou an example unto the brethren in all things. Keep thyself pure."

Note the four o'clock start, at which time I am often praying for you, and request that you would do the same for me at that hour. Believe me, you lay near my heart, and nothing but sin shall ever part thy soul and mine.

In October of the same year, he again writes Mr. Fidler, who seems to have been anxious to receive an appointment to Shelburne, and had requested his friend to speak to Mr. Black with a view to having such appointment made. Mr. Jessop says: "All this and a great deal more I would willingly do for you, my dear brother; but this I cannot do with a clear conscience under present circumstances of things." The circumstances to which he refers were: Mr. Boyd, who had been laboring in New Brunswick, had concluded to locate himself, and there was a loud call for Mr. Fidler's services on the circuit up the river, that "hundreds of constant hearers, as well as many members of our society, are suffering for the want of preaching; therefore, if ever you were wanting on any place it is here at present. Dear brother, come on with all speed (leaving your every concern with the Lord), full of faith and the Holy Ghost, and may the God of the seas deliver you and bring you safe over to us again with flying colours before a glorious wind. I shall expect you, without any doubt, by the return of Brother Humbert's vessel. I have just returned from Passamaquoddy, down the Bay of Fundy, and have been travelling and preaching until I am almost worn out, but glory to God, I am laboring for a good Master, whose pay is sure. Brother Boyd says he considers it to be his duty to take care of his family; to do which he thinks it best to locate himself, and to go into business. He intends keeping a school this winter, and in the spring to go into the mercantile business. So it is,—the devil tells us, when about to marry, that it will not hinder our travelling, but in the end to our sorrow, we find him a liar; wherefore, if we want to travel, the best way is to live single. Many people give it as their opinion that there is a loadstone to the eastward as well as to the westward ———."

Another letter was from the Rev. William Grandin, dated Annapolis, 13th March, 1795, in which he says that the Lord had greatly blessed his work there, and sending his love to his friends at Sheffield, St. Ann's, and the Nashwaak, assuring them that, as the Lord was his witness, he loved them. He also makes mention of Mr. Boyd, to whom he had lent thirty out of his forty shillings of quarterage.

There are two letters from Stephen Humbert, one written in 1795, the other in 1797; in the latter he says: "I bless God, since I saw you last I have found it my hearty desire and purpose to cleave unto the Lord, and though many hindrances strew all the way, yet many are the comforts and great the encouragements of those that trust in Him. Our society affairs are not the most promising here. We have had but little stirring among the people. Some few have become serious; a few have been added, and those that profess faith are in general growing stronger."

Rev. James Mann, writing to Mr. Fidler from New York, says: "Am happy to hear that the state of religion in Saint John is better than my fears, for Mr. Jessop had written so discouragingly concerning it, I expected scarcely four families had remained in the society. I labored hard and long in Saint

John, and hope not altogether without fruit, and still retain a frugal regard for that people,—however, I may be forgotten by them. Whether ever I shall see them again is at present hard for me to determine, but hope that they may not be left to be picked up by apostate Methodists nor antinomain innovators." He then makes a reference to Mr. Boyd, the publicity to which would serve no purpose, and also exhibits anxiety as to the appointments for the year, and remarks : "I have received no advice from any of the preachers since conference, but yourself, owing, I imagine, to the want of conveyance. Where is Brother Wilson and Brother McColl? What has become of a young man up the river by the name of McCloud; does he exhort? Where is my dear old friend, Brother Davis? Has he forgot me? Religion is low in this city. Republican principles and politics eat it out of many hearts." Mr. McCloud, mentioned above, was Alexander McLeod, already referred to and whose name will receive further mention.

The other letters are from Rev. William Black, and, owing to his relation to the society and the ministers at that time as superintendent, they will be given almost in full. In the first, dated Windsor, June 8th, 1795, he says: "I am exceedingly sorry it was not in your power to be with us at the conference. We have, however, made out as well as we could without you and Brother Jessop; and thought best that you should take your station again in New Brunswick. You must change with Brother McColl as is most convenient, and labor in the city or the country as shall be most for the good of the people. You, possibly, may change with Brother Wilson in the winter or early the next spring, or,—if you desire it and it is in my power to effect it,—with some other preacher, perhaps Mr. Grandin."

The stations in Nova Scotia and New Brunswick, for that year, were:

Halifax — William Black, } These to change this summer.
Newport — John Mann,
Cumberland — Benjamin Wilson.
Liverpool — James Mann.
Shelburne — Richard Stocket.
New Brunswick — D. Fidler and D. McColl.

The second letter, dated Halifax, September 23rd, 1795: " Your letter received, enclosing one to Mr. Smith, for which I had to pay double postage, viz., one shilling and five pence. I would have written to you sooner only I wished to avoid writing to you by post. It cost me three shillings in two days the last week for letters. I suppose by this time Mr. James Mann is with you. I wish, if the circumstances of things with you require it, he may tarry with you. I do not know how I can help you at present by sending you a preacher. I have just received a letter from Bishop Asbury, and another from Jesse Lee. They complain much of the dulness of the work in the States. The bishop appears to be in painful exercise about it. He also remarks to me that the young men who have returned from us to the States are not so humble and serious as when they went to Nova Scotia. This, my dear brother, may suggest a useful head of self-examination for you. I hope he will not have to make a like observation concerning you at your return to them. I will thank you to let me know how you come on, — at least once a quarter. What number of friends remain in the city of Saint John? Are they able to keep a preacher? I have been informed they are not. The work of God in England is said to be astonishing. Hallelujah? Amen. It is a dull time here and in most parts of the Province; nothing seems to be doing. You have my prayers that God may bless you in your soul and labors."

The third letter is dated at Saint John, July 28th, 1798,

and is addressed to Mr. Fidler, who was then in Halifax. He says : " After a tedious passage of seven days our vessel put into Mahogany, where I obtained a horse and rode to Carleton. On my arrival at Saint John, I found Mr. McColl and Mr. Wilson waiting for me; and was glad that I had been so providentially prevented from proceeding to Saint Stephen. The next day we had our little conference, and could see no plan more eligible than that Mr. McColl should take his station at the city and Brother Wilson his at Cumberland; and so request Brother Fidler to spend the winter at Saint Stephen, where I am persuaded he will find himself much more happily situated than at Cumberland. In the spring you can change with Brother McColl, if you choose so to do. After my arrival at Halifax, you may either proceed from Windsor directly to St. Stephen, or call awhile at the city and see your old friends. The former will be less expensive; the latter, perhaps, more pleasing. Christian prudence must direct, and providence open the way. I will thank you to remember me to my dear friends at Halifax, as if particularly named. I seldom know how much I am attached to them until I am for a time separated from them. I trust God will bless your public and private labors amongst them to your mutual edification and comfort. I have not yet learned anything respecting Brother James Mann. I feel and fear for Barrington in this unprotected state. Oh, that the merciful Shepherd of souls would keep them from the prowling wolf. Mr. Boyd has removed with his family to the States, —I believe somewhere not far from Portland. Mr. McColl has gone to Sheffield. Brother Wilson will go off for Cumberland, by land, in two or three days. I have preached once, viz., last evening, to a pretty large number. To-morrow, 1 trust, will be a day of holy rest and sweet employment. We hope our Master's royal presence will make our hearts glad ! We are far from you, but hope our prayers will meet yours at the throne of grace and acceptance, where smiling mercy bestows her donations and answers the requests of needy supplicants; where the good Samaritan binds up the hearts, the wounded, broken hearts of conscious sinners, and makes the lame to leap for joy. Come on, beloved, draw us and we will cheerfully run after Thee. Amen. Do not forget to pray for your affectionate brother and fellow-laborer in the kingdom and patience of Jesus Christ."

The fourth letter is also written from Saint John, dated 22nd August, 1798, in which he says: "As Mr. Humbert, who bears this to you, intends spending two or three weeks in Halifax, I think you had best avail yourself of his horse and make the best of your way to Windsor,—perhaps you may be there in time to come here by the return of the brig in which he takes his passage from home. There may not be another opportunity soon, as the paris plaster becomes every day of less and less value. In case he should go to Halifax, according to his present intention, I can stay a week or two longer here, where there appears a prospect of good being done. I wrote to you some time ago, acquainting you that it was thought by the preachers here advisable that you should go to Saint Stephen, rather than to Cumberland. I am persuaded it will be more for your comfort. I hope the change is of God and will answer the best of purposes,— your comfort, the benefit of souls and the glory of God."

The last letter is written from Saint John, dated August 31st, 1798. He says: "As there is a considerable stir here, both within and without the society, I am solicitously requested by many, with prayers and tears, not to leave Saint John at this time; have, therefore, for fear I should do wrong, concluded it best for me to tarry awhile,—at least until I can hear from you. What your feelings may be respecting your going to the States this fall, I cannot tell; you must know best. This, however, is notorious, if you go away this fall the work in this Province must suffer. I believe you love God, and are concerned for the interest of souls, and think, I may venture to conclude, your next letter will inform me that however desirous you are of seeing your friends in the States, you will deny yourself that pleasure for the present and wait for an opportunity when your lack of service will be less unfriendly to the interests of religion in this connection. Let me have your full conclusion so as when I write to Brother McColl, on my leaving this city, I may know what directions to give. You can then, on my return, come to this city on your way to Saint Stephen, or go directly there as inclination or opportunity may lead. If you desire it, Mr. McColl will change with you early in the spring, and you can take your stand awhile in this city or up the river. After your arrival here, you can go to Saint Stephen sooner or later this fall, as conviction of duty may lead, when you and Mr. McColl come together."

The above extracts are given for several reasons: They were written by men whom we delight to honor. They were written either from Saint John, or addressed to Saint John, and in several instances have a direct bearing upon the state of the society at that time. They disclose the simplicity in which the affairs of the infant church were administered. They show the stamp of the humble men who gave Methodism its start, and by comparison they most assuredly show that in its development the hand of God has been its guide during all the years.

The conference of the United States continued to supply missionaries for the Provinces until 1799, but from one cause and another they soon returned home. It became evident that if success was to be achieved there must be a more steady and permanent supply. Accordingly Mr. Black went to England to solicit from the Wesleyan conference several missionaries. In his efforts he was supported by Dr. Coke, and the conference consented that four preachers should be sent out with Mr. Black to labor in British North America. These were Messrs. Lowry, Bennet, Marsden and Oliphant. They arrived in Halifax on the 4th October, 1800, after a tedious passage of six weeks. Three of these young men, succeeding each other from time to time, labored in Saint John for eight years. Mr. Oliphant being first appointed to the charge, and continued in it for two years, being succeeded by Mr. Marsden, who ministered in 1802-03. On the second day of June, 1802, Messrs. Marsden and Bennet, having gone to New York, were duly ordained as deacons and elders in the Methodist Episcopal Church by Bishops Whatcoat and Asbury. Mr. Bennet was appointed to Saint John for the years 1803-04, and was followed by Mr. Marsden, who remained on the circuit for four years.

These early ministers performed a vast amount of work and suffered much privation. They were missionaries in the true sense. They were in it because they felt called to it. Their salary was £16 a year, exclusive of board. One week they would lodge with one family and the next with another, paying, therefore, six shillings and six pence, while they would pursue a system of daily itineracy in reference to their dinners.

In any paper having reference to the early history of Methodism in Saint John, no matter what the temptation to hurry on may be, the name of Joshua Marsden should not be lightly passed over. The less excuse is there, because in an intensely interesting but very rare little book entitled, "The Narrative of a Mission," Mr. Marsden has left an account of his labors in the Provinces. The narrative is given in a series of letters, forty-seven in all, which are addressed to James Montgomery. The copy used by the writer is the property of the New Brunswick Historical Society. The opportunity to peruse the book can now be enjoyed by so few persons, that it is felt desirable to make extended extracts therefrom so far as they relate to Saint John. Some might be disposed to resent his references to the scenery and climate, but then they must bear in mind that the Saint John of 1889 is very different from the city of which he wrote, nor was the protection against cold as perfect and complete as it is in our day.

From a passport issued to Mr. Marsden in 1814, it would appear that he was five feet eight inches high, was about thirty-six years of age and light complexion, brown hair and blue eyes. Having arrived in this country in the year 1800, he would, therefore, be twenty-two years of age when he began his ministry. He says: "The city of Saint John, the theatre of my present mission, is situated at the mouth of the river of the same name; it is on the western side of the Bay of Fundy, in latitude 45 degrees north and about 65 degrees 30 minutes west longitude. The town, or city, for it has a royal charter, is but fifty years old. It has neither beauty of form, nor loveliness of situation to recommend it; all around it is sterile and barren, and nothing could have recommended so unsightly a spot but its being at the mouth of this fine river which pours its produce down into the Bay of Fundy. The town contains about five or six hundred houses, with a population of three or four thousand inhabitants, who are chiefly employed in mercantile, timber and fishing speculations. If we except the Church and the Wesleyan Mission Chapel, it cannot boast of many public buildings. There are also in the town a courthouse, on the hill barracks for the soldiers, and an academy. The river is wide, and has a noble fishery for salmon, shad, herring and sturgeon,--which furnishes employment and wealth to more than two-thirds of the inhabitants. The tide in the river rises nearly forty feet, a circumstance that renders the Bay of Fundy famous throughout the world. It rolls along these shores with a majesty and grandeur I never saw in any other place; and in some parts of the bay with a rapidity of current from seven to nine miles an hour. Two miles from the city, are the falls of the river,—a body of water nearly a mile wide and from twenty to thirty feet in depth, is all at once compressed between a bed of rocks, which frown over its roaring waters, and through which it rushes with an impetuosity and violence no language can possibly describe. The descent is about twenty feet; the noise is terrible, and gives something like a tremulous motion to all the surrounding scenery. It covers the whole harbor of Saint John with foam and froth, and spreads a hollow roaring noise for several miles around. Mighty Father, how grand and sublime are Thy works! At what period did this spacious river burst through this wall of granite, and tear in sunder the stupendous cliffs by which it is overhung? Round the city for several miles, nothing either beautiful or charming attracts the eye; the whole scenery is rocky, barren and forbidding,—hence whoever travels through the western world to behold verdant scenery, and lovely prospects, must avoid the neighborhood of Saint John, where the whole landscape unites an assemblage of the most dreary traits of nature that the traveller could select. Here are irregular clumps of stunted spruce growing among the rocks; salt marshes bounded by jutting and fearful crags; muddy creeks, where swarms of pestiferous musquitos annoy the neighboring inhabitants."

Mr. Marsden then describes other portions of his circuit, which extended up the Saint John river, taking in Fredericton, as well as other distant points. The object in making the extract already transferred to this paper, is to show the obstacles and discouragements with which our early missionaries had to contend. Notwithstanding the rigidity of the New Brunswick winter, Mr. Marsden ought to have been comfortable, as, he says, his dress was as follows: "Woollen stockings and socks underneath; over my boots and underdress, a large pair of thick woollen socks shod at the feet with leather, and reaching to the upper part of the thigh; a surtout coat, and over this a fear-naught; on the hands, worsted or lambswool gloves, and over them thick mittens; a fur cap, with a large silk handkerchief tied around the lower part of my face. * * * * * I found in the city a lively and united little church, and entered upon my labors among them with much comfort. They were few in number, but warm hearted and zealous; and as I had to go from house to house to get my food, I had soon an opportunity of becoming personally acquainted with each individual. Besides the whites in the society, we had a number of free blacks,—some of whom were truly pious, and greatly helped me by their prayers. I found much prejudice existing in the place, which even the piety of that angel of humanity, Mr. Bishop, had not been able to subdue; yet my poor labors, if not remarkably successful at first, were in the end greatly blessed; and I ploughed and sowed in hope. Our little chapel (for we did not erect another for several years after this period), was greatly crowded, and both blacks and whites were very attentive and much quickened. During the winter 1804–5, I labored in Saint John and along the banks of the river with visible success and much satisfaction. Old differences in the society were composed and the contending parties reconciled. Among the town's people prejudice seemed to lose ground. There was a manifest increase of Christian affection and simplicity among the society. With regard to myself, I speak in the fear of God, my soul was much alive, and my affections were warmed with holy desire to promote the glory of my blessed Redeemer and the salvation of His moral family. I divided the day into regular parts. I rose every morning in the bitterest weather at four o'clock, and lighted a fire in the stove, as this only would warm the room and check the intense cold. From four till eight I devoted my time to meditation and prayer, reading and writing. The forenoon I spent in going from house to house among the society and congregation and visiting the sick. The afternoon was taken up in reading and meeting the classes,—four of which I regularly met every week; and in the evening, throughout the whole winter, we had generally a meeting of one kind or another. I held prayer meetings in different parts of the town, and as the intense cold prevented me from preaching in the chapel, I preached from house to house. Once a week I catechised the children, and every Monday evening had a select meeting at my own house for reading the lives and experience of Christians. As the spring opened my trials increased. I was led to deal very faithfully with my congregations. I had to preach against Sabbath breaking, and the magistrates thought that I reflected upon their conduct, because,—during the herring, salmon and shad season,—they allowed the people to fish upon the Lord's day, and assigned as a reason that fish ran more abundantly on that day than any other. But they were merchants, and bought the fish, and sordid interest will never want a plea for breaking in upon the most sacred duties. Dancing and revelling prevailed in an unusual degree; I had to take notice of these,—hence some of the gay ones, who occasionally came to the chapel, thought themselves implicated and came no more. Conscience and duty required me to preach against drunkenness, and as this was the besetting sin in the place, 'Master, by so saying thou condemnest us,' was felt by a number of delinquents. I had to animadvert upon smuggling, and this came home to the very doors of the Church of God; an official brother possessing some property and more influence, would hardly speak of me with charity or treat me with common civility. Ah! this preaching against sin, when you know your congregation are committing it; here's the rub, especially should they be rich and obstinate. Can you double this cape? Can you steer boldly forward in these broken waters? There is the Scylla of God's wrath if you neglect your duty; here is the Chyribdis of man's displeasure if you are faithful. Notwithstanding all my discouragements the little mission greatly flourished. A part of the society in the city of Saint John consisted of black people; two of whom by their holy and circumspect lives, were a great blessing to the rest, and much esteemed by all the congregation. The names of these were Jonas Murdock and Libbe Weeks. Libbe was one of the most pious and gifted negresses I ever knew; her talents were as remarkable as her zeal, and her fervour and eloquence in prayer rendered her a singular blessing to many. I gave her permission to conduct prayer meetings among her own color, and to meet the class of black people belonging to the chapel."

In the autumn of 1804, Mr. Black, in a letter to the missionary committee in London, says: "At the city of Saint John our chapel will probably contain four hundred persons, and is generally well attended. There are about eighty in the society, our members here have been much reduced by emigration, occasioned chiefly by the late and present war having so seriously affected their trade."

To return to Mr. Marsden's narrative, he says: "During the winter of 1805, the mission in Saint John flourished exceedingly. We had a number of awakenings, and in the midst of a most severe season much life, harmony and love. The cold was, indeed, intense and the snow was nearly six feet deep." The descriptions of the storms, the intense cold and great suffering of that winter are omitted, as well as accounts of his journeys on the river and Grand Lake, and also much that is largely of a personal character. "Our covenant meeting held in Saint John, on the beginning of the year 1806, was the most powerful I had ever attended; so great was the Holy One in the midst of us that an emotion of solemn awe, mixed with astonishment and self-abasing humility, was evidently felt by many hearts. * * * The Lord was with us of a truth, and with all I suffered from the cold by travelling in open sleds, or sleeping in log huts, I never recollect those days, but I wish to live them over again; they were some of the happiest of my life. I prayed three times a day with my wife and family, also frequently in secret, and in every company I strove to introduce something spiritual."

At the end of the year Mr. Marsden visited parts of his mission on the Saint John river, intending to be absent about a month. The little flock and congregation in the city were left in charge of the leaders and a local brother who supplied his place in the pulpit. A little after his departure they held a watch night service, which was attended with some unusual tokens of a quickening and reviving nature, and was followed up by a series of protracted services in which the people were wonderfully blessed. When he returned home the brethren flocked to his house to inform him of what had taken place and to make preparation for further work. He says: "Such a stir in religion was quite a new thing in Saint John. Some wondered whereunto it would grow; others condemned the whole as enthusiasm and delusion. A few respectable persons in the congregation took great offence and requested that I would put a stop to the dangerous wild-fire that was spreading in the society. Complaint was made to Mr. Campbell, the mayor, who said he did not doubt but that Mr. Marsden would soon put it down. The things that appeared most out of the ordinary way were praising God aloud, crying for mercy, children exhorting, several praying at the same time, and holding the meetings until twelve o'clock at night,— nay, upon a few occasions until two or three in the morning, although I generally dismissed them myself about ten o'clock. * * * In this revival there was little of what may be termed wildfire or extravagance in expression; although numbers cried aloud for mercy there was no clapping of hands and shouting. The whole town, which is but small, felt the influence; an air of morality pervaded it and the profaneness of the streets was greatly diminished. A great and visible change had taken place in many persons and this even the proud opposers of the work could not deny; yet they thought, or affected to think, it was all sham and pretence and would vanish into smoke. One of the principal enemies of the work, who got some doggerel verses printed in handbills and circulated through the town, came to nothing and was obliged to fly from the place in disgrace. Old bickerings were done away and much love and harmony prevailed in the society. Prior to this awakening the society consisted of about ninety members. One hundred new members were added to the society in the space of a month, which, in a place containing about three thousand inhabitants, is no inconsiderable proportion.

"During the summer of 1807 I devoted much of my time and attention to the great object of erecting in the city of Saint John a new mission chapel. For, ever since the revival of the work of God, both the society and the congregation had so much increased that the old chapel was too small to contain them. In this work, however, I was greatly discouraged,— many of the society were in indigent circumstances, and we had not, as in the case at present, home resources to assist us. The few I consulted gave me little encouragement. Having, however, with some difficulty persuaded several friends to assist me in this blessed work, we first bought a piece of land near the new church (Trinity), and then procured a frame or skeleton for a building sixty feet long by forty-two wide. The congregation and society volunteered their services, and on a day appointed we dug the foundation. Many of the inhabitants of the town with a generous zeal, lent us their carts and horses to drag stone, others assisted us to bring the frame of the building from the river side, to which it had been rafted down from the upper woods; and after I had preached on the foundation stone, more than one hundred able-bodied men came forward to enable us to raise the frame. At this building I worked with my own hands from morning till night for several months, as an example to induce and encourage others, and also because my heart was in the work and the Lord gave me strength for the day: so that I know not that ever I was better in body or happier in soul than when I worked all day at the new and preached at night in the old chapel."

Mr. Marsden does not mention the text from which he preached at the laying of the foundation stone. It was, however, "Upon this rock I will build my church, and the gates of hell shall not prevail against it." Nor does he give the names of any of the friends who assisted him in the enterprise. As we pass, reference should be made especially to John Ferguson, one of the earliest converts in the city, of whom more will be said in another place. Some of the townspeople of that day laughed at the band of praying Methodists attempting an enterprise which seemed so hazardous. Mr. Ferguson tells us that "as they passed the building they would look up and sneeringly say, 'That will never be finished!'" The church was completed in the following year, and on Christmas day, 1808, dedicated. Mr. Marsden having been removed to Bermuda, the sermon was preached and the dedicatory services conducted by Rev. William Bennet.

The cut on the opposite page represents the old Germain street church and parsonage as they appeared immediately before their destruction in the great fire of 1877.

THE GERMAIN STREET CHURCH AND PARSONAGE.

There are still living in our city a few persons who remember the building of the old Germain street chapel. Mr. James Bustin, who is now eighty-eight years of age, said to the writer, "The remembrance of that old church was very dear to me. When a small boy I played around its foundation. Saw the structure rise, and with boyish interest watched for its completion. In this church I worshipped over sixty years." Mrs. John Humbert, who is a sister of Mr. Bustin, is also among those who remember the erection of the old chapel.

Rev. William Black was appointed for the second time to the city, succeeding Mr. Bennet, and remained two years. In the early part of his term the first Sabbath School in Saint John was formed. He distinguished himself by an able defence of Methodism in answer to certain insulting articles which appeared in the Saint John *Gazette*. He was followed by Stephen Bamford, who was held in the highest respect and was welcome wherever he went. He had been in the army for fourteen years. In 1806, three years after obtaining his discharge, he entered the ministry and for thirty years labored with great acceptance. During the last twelve years of his life he was a supernumary. Dr. McLeod says of him, "that upon entering their house his usual salutation was, 'Here is Stephen Bamford again!' accompanied by some witty remark. He was an original wit, and I have known him to make his audience laugh and cry in the time of a few minutes. One anecdote I remember, and have heard my parents frequently repeat it. Preaching to sinners, he said: 'Some of you when the last trump shall sound, will be glad to take hold of Stephen Bamford's coat tail, but I will not let you. I'll wear a round jacket.' I have seen various versions of this incident and attributed to different ministers, but I believe it originated with Mr. Bamford,—it occurred nearly eighty years ago. Many of Mr.

Bamford's sayings are still repeated. He would often appeal to his wife, from the pulpit, to corroborate something he had said. He was the most interesting exhorter I ever heard,—always something fresh, appropriate and improving. He was a true Christian, upright and honorable to an extreme, lived well and died well." Mr. Bamford possessed naturally an active and vigorous mind, which he improved by valuable reading and careful and accurate observation of men and things. His best characteristics were that he was a man of strong faith, of earnest prayer and of a grateful spirit.

Although a supernumary, he continued to preach every Sabbath. While at Digby in the year 1843 his horse ran away, injuring seriously both himself and Mrs. Bamford. He gives an account in the Methodist magazine for that year of his injuries, and a postcript to his letter, written a fortnight later, illustrates the zeal and earnestness of purpose of this man of God. He says: "The leg still remains helpless. Preach every Sabbath. They carry me to the chapel and God blesses me. Write by the bearer and let me know all the news. My health is good, and my soul is growing more happy as I approach nearer to eternity! O Religion! O Methodism! What do I owe you? What I never can repay!!" His end was peace. He died at Digby, N. S., August 14th, 1848, in the seventy-eighth year of his age, and the forty-second of his ministry,—and was buried in the Methodist burial ground of this city. Mr. Bamford was the last minister sent from the lower provinces to the United States for ordination.

Reference has been made to the Sabbath school formed in the summer of 1809, during Mr. Black's pastorate. It was organized by Mr. George Taylor, a school master and local preacher of much acceptance; a gentleman most active in Christian work and one who was well and favorably known to many of our people still living. This was the first Sabbath school established in Saint John. Mr. James Bustin, already referred to, was a member of it. Mrs. Humbert, his sister, was not, for the reason that girls were not admitted.

During Mr. Bamford's incumbency the following notice and appeal in reference to this school, was published :

SUNDAY SCHOOL, GERMAIN STREET.

The public are respectfully informed that children are admitted into the school, as usual, every Sabbath day at two o'clock. It being now nearly three years since any subscriptions having been received for its support, the managers beg leave to solicit the assistance of all who are well-wishers to such a useful and laudable institution; at the same time are informed that any aid they may be pleased to afford will be thankfully received by the Rev. Stephen Bamford, or John Ferguson.

STATEMENT OF FINANCES.

Amount of subscriptions received since the commencement of the school.....................	£17 10s. 7d.
Deduct disbursements for fuel, books, slates, pencils, etc..	16 16 0
Balance remaining on hand................	£0 14s. 7d.

SAINT JOHN, N. B., September 10th, 1812.

The charge for disbursements indicates in a measure the nature of Sabbath school instruction in that day, in comparison with which the present teaching is in marked contrast.

Mr. Bustin says : "The boys assembled in the morning at the Sabbath school room (the old chapel), in time to be arranged for marching to church under the direction of one or more of the teachers. In the afternoon the school was opened with prayer and scripture reading, after which the boys were classed off for spelling, reading, writing and cyphering. The writing was inspected and the calculations were corrected by the superintendent and teachers." Ten minutes would be occupied at the close of the session by one of the teachers in enforcing some moral or religious truth. Mr. Taylor was assisted in his work by William Till, Isaac Goodwin, Alexander McLeod and others.

In the year 1812, the town clock was placed in position in Trinity church tower,—before that date much difficulty was experienced in assembling people at a certain hour, and so much latitude was allowed that neither was punctuality nor procrastination regarded as the thief of time. The Episcopalians had service in the morning only, and, of course, their bell would be silent in the evening. It was regarded as a great innovation on the part of the Methodists to have an evening service. They were brought together by the announcement that the service would begin at early candle light. It was the day of "penny dips," nor was the the luxury of carpets on the church floors known. The necessary continual snuffing of the candles, and the steady tramp of the sexton during the entire service, while attending to that duty must have seriously disturbed the order and solemnity of the occasion.

In 1813, Rev. James Knowlan succeeded Mr. Bamford and remained in Saint John for two years. He lived in a house at the head of "Cooper's alley" (Church street), next door to Mr. McLeod's. He was always spoken well of,—was a good, sound Methodist preacher.

In 1815, William Croscombe was assigned to Saint John. Mr. Croscombe's fame is in all the churches in New Brunswick, Nova Scotia and (what was formerly called) Canada. A devoted, zealous, energetic man of God,—very successful in winning souls to Christ and in building up believers in faith and holiness. He was beloved by the people and held in the highest esteem. He was a valuable correspondent to the *Wesleyan*, ever alert to defend Methodism when attacked or misrepresented, as the files of that paper abundantly show. Loved in life, he was mourned in death.

Mr. Bamford, in 1817, followed Mr. Croscombe and was stationed for the second time in the city, remaining two years, and was succeeded by James Priestly, who labored from 1819 to 1821. Mr. Priestly is said to have been a most winning preacher, and was certainly held in highest esteem by many of the people. By some others he was looked upon as a plagiarist having great resource to Jay's short sermons, but not by any regarded as a man without wonderful ability.

In 1821, Robert Alder was appointed to Saint John. He had been a printer in early life, but was received on trial in the Methodist ministry in 1816. He was medium sized, but compact. His head was very large and surmounted by very curly hair. His preaching was elaborate, dignified and powerful. When stationed in Saint John no minister was more popular. Such congregations for numbers and intelligent hearers drawn from all quarters, had, up to that time, never been seen in old Germain street chapel. Rev. Dr. Burns, the Presbyterian clergyman at that time in the city, was a frequent attendant at the Sunday evening preaching. Mr. Alder subsequently occupied the principal appointments in what was then known as Canada. He became at length one of the secretaries of our missionary society and one of the most prominent men in the British conference. At the time of his death, however, he was not a member of the Methodist society. He remained in Saint John until 1823, when, for a second time, Mr. Priestly was stationed in the city.

In this year trouble began, the most serious, perhaps, our church in its history has had. Through the kindness of J. W. Lawrence, Esq., an extended account of what was known as the "Priestly affair," is here presented:

"Rev. Mr. Priestly was in charge of the Germain street

church in 1824. He was an able preacher and much liked by his congregation. In person, Mr. Priestly was tall and on the sunny side of forty years. In the spring of that year at a meeting of the Methodist district, held in Nova Scotia, Rev. William Bennet being chairman and Rev. Robert Alder secretary, Mr. Priestly's name was arrested and a charge brought against him of indulging in the drinking customs of the day to a degree incompatible with the position of a minister. At this time there were only four Methodist stations in New Brunswick,—Saint John, Fredericton, St. Stephen and Sackville, to which Rev. Robert Alder, Rev. John Marshall, Rev. D. McColl, and Rev. S. Bamford were respectively stationed. At the district meeting Mr. Priestly was not present. The district decided that the wisest course was for Mr. Priestly to resign his charge at Saint John, go to England and explain his position to the London conference, from which body he received his appointment. Upon the advice of his friends he declined to act on the suggestion entirely, but resigned his pastorate. It was at this time Mr. Priestly's wife died, leaving three young children, which deepened the general sympathy for him. On the 31st July in the same year, a meeting of his friends was held at his residence, at which Stephen Humbert, Daniel Ansley, Barzilla Bailey, John McClure, David Brown and Alexander Miller were appointed a committee to obtain subscriptions for the erection of a place of worship. So popular was the movement that on the 14th August, only two weeks' after, two lots facing King Square were purchased, and seven days later the corner stone of what was thereafter to be termed the Asylum chapel was laid. On the Sunday evening following a sermon was preached on the ground by Mr. Priestly, when a collection of £18 was taken. At a public meeting in the Masonic Hall, at the head of King street, a gold medal was presented to Mr. Priestly by citizens irrespective of creed. The presentation committee was Nehemiah Merritt, Stephen Humbert, Lewis Burns and John R. Partelow. In October a circus visited Saint John and gave a benefit for the building fund, realizing $111. 'So the carpenter encouraged the goldsmith, and he that smoothed with the hammer him that smote the anvil, saying it is ready for the soldering, and he fasteneth it with nails that it should not be moved.' So rapidly did the work go forward that on Sunday, December 12th, less than four months after laying the corner stone, the building was opened for worship and a collection taken of £38."

In May, 1825, Stephen Humbert, a leading Methodist and head in the movement in behalf of Mr. Priestly, wrote:

"The Asylum chapel was erected the latter part of last summer. It is built of yellow brick and forms a handsome exterior, and intended for the reception of Rev. James Priestly, who officiated as pastor a few months only and was dismissed on a charge of conduct unfitting a minister. The chapel is an ornament to the city and will abide as a lasting testimony of the benevolence of the inhabitants of Saint John. The trustees are corresponding with the president of the conference of Primitive Methodists, at Home generally called Church of England Methodists, in contradistinction to the Wesleyan Methodists, who have separated from the ordinances administered in the Church of England. An eminent minister is soon expected from the old country."

Mr. Priestly shortly afterwards left for Canada, where misfortunes seemed to follow him to the close of life.

The Rev. George Montgomery West, of the Episcopal Methodist church, arrived on a visit from Canada, preaching his first sermon in the Asylum chapel, July 5th, 1825. Mr. West was of commanding presence and possessed pulpit attainments of a high order, drawing large audiences. On the 24th July the pews on the ground floor were sold, realizing £500. The building faced the square, and unlike churches generally, its frontage was longer than the depth,—one advantage of which was, there being ground on the rear an enlargement could be made and would add to its general appearance. There were one end and two side galleries.

Mr. West's stay was short, for a minister of his gifts could command a wider field. He preached his last sermon October 14th, only three months after his arrival. It was for the benefit of the sufferers from the Miramichi fire. A collection was taken at this service amounting to £40.

Rev. Richard Robinson, sent by the Irish conference of Primitive Methodists, arrived in this city on October 9th, 1825. The interest in the new movement had largely passed. Numbers returned to the Germain Street Methodist Church and others went to the Stone (Episcopal) Church, opened in 1826. Mr. Robinson not finding things as prosperous as he expected, returned to Ireland. He was succeeded by Rev. Mr. Ashley, followed by Mr. Parent, neither of whom was able to sustain the movement, and the end was the closing of the Asylum chapel in connection with Methodism."

The building has an interesting subsequent history, particulars of which Mr. Lawrence has preserved. We may state that from 1831 to the fall of 1835 it was in the occupation of the Episcopalians, who, under the ministry of Rev. B. G. Gray, rector of Trinity, held what were called Free Evening Services on each Sabbath. It was also used for Sunday school purposes and for the meetings of the Bible Society, as well as for quarterly meetings of a temperance society whose platform was wine and ale admissable, while strong drinks had no quarter. In 1835 a number of members of Saint Andrew's Kirk purchased the chapel, and it became known as Saint Stephen's church, and the organization now known by the latter name was formed. In 1847 the Legislature passed an act authorizing the sale of the building. The proceeds, after payment of debts, were to be applied to the erection of a church in accord with the Established Church of Scotland. In 1848 Saint David's church was organized in this building.

Mr. Lawrence, in concluding a paper read before the Historical Society, entitled "A Building with a History," says: "Such is the brief outline of an edifice which has had a more chequered history than any in Saint John, and the history of the watchman on its battlements, fighting the world, the flesh and the devil. That the world, the flesh and the devil were the victors the conviction is irresistible, when it is recalled that James Priestly, William Anderson and Thomas Wishart were ejected from the fortress by those who placed them there. The days of its triumphs were, when used for Church of England service, and when it became the birthplace and cradle of Saint David's."

This unfortunate circumstance was a serious blow for the time being to Methodism in Saint John, and the exercise of much wisdom was necessary in the selection of some one for the work of repairing the injury done. None more competent could have been chosen than Mr. Alder, and he was accordingly appointed to the charge. His first congregation did not number thirty; but he gained each Sunday, and finally the sad confirmation of the action of the district being established by the notorious conduct of Mr. Priestly, the people in great numbers returned to the old house and the adherents became more numerous and the cause more prosperous than before the downfall.

It should be remembered that Mr. McLeod and others of the leading Methodists were subjected to much persecution because,—acting from principle and a sense of Christian duty,—they felt obliged to urge a strict enforcement of the discipline against Mr. Priestly, and bear witness to his intemperate habits before a special district meeting.

The newspapers of that day contain many attacks upon these gentlemen, principally, as usual, by anonymous writers, but in some instances over individual signatures. By reference to the columns of the *Courier*, for instance, this will be made manifest.

Mr. McLeod at this time was the leading Methodist in the city, and as an official member of the church he rendered much valuable assistance for many years. His house on Germain, near Church street, was the home of the Methodist minister. His counsel determined their course in many matters. In early life it had been his intention to enter the ministry, but later on he had some doubts as to his call, and subsequently he again resolved to enter the work. Having offered, he was about to depart for the conference, but meeting with an accident on the morning of his intended departure, the interruption probably changed the whole course of his life. In Saint John he rendered much assistance as a local preacher and a class-leader. On the 29th April, 1815, he retired from school teaching, and from that time devoted his attention to mercantile life and literary pursuits of another character than teaching. From 1826 until 1831 he was editor and proprietor of the *City Gazette*. In 1829 he started the *New Brunswick Religious and Literary Journal*, which was probably the first religious paper or periodical published in the Province, and which existed about two years. Mr. McLeod was prominent in the temperance and other moral movements, and was the first secretary of the first Temperance Society in Saint John, Rev. Dr. Gray being president and Rev. Dr. Burns vice president. This society was organized in 1829. Mr. McLeod's place of business, No. 4 South wharf, was the depository of the Bible Society. He died 28th March, 1833, aged sixty years, at the time of his death he was Coroner and County Treasurer. His wife, two sons and one daughter survived him. Mrs. McLeod died in 1838, her funeral taking place on Good Friday in that year. His daughter was the wife of Rev. Albert Desbrisay, who, though a great sufferer during the most of her life, was of gentle and sweet disposition, a woman of strong mental endowment and kindly remembered by all with whom she was acquainted. His son, Mr. J. Wesley McLeod, resided in Saint John for a number of years, was actively connected with the Methodist Society, and is most favorably remembered by the older citizens of this place. He died a few years ago in New Jersey. Rev. A. W. McLeod, D. D., the other son, entered the ministry with Rev. Henry Daniel and Rev. George Johnston in the year 1830, but since 1854 has been residing in the United States and now lives at Baltimore, Md. To Dr. McLeod the writer is indebted for much that appears in this paper. Of himself he, in a letter written in July, 1889, says: "I am now past eighty-one years of age, but can read the smallest print, and write without the aid of spectacles, and am by no means deficient in activity; * * above all I feel an abiding interest in Christ and can witness a good confession. I am conscious that I am living on borrowed time and my chief solicitude is, to be found ready when the Master calls."

PORTLAND.

Occasional visits were made to Portland and Indiantown by the Wesleyan missionaries stationed in the city. These were the more frequent during the superintendence of Rev. Richard Williams, who was appointed to the station in 1826. The services were usually held in the house of Mr. J. Owens, which was always open for that purpose. So promising was the field that it was soon thought proper to build a chapel.

An eligible site having been presented by the Hon. Charles Simonds, the enterprise was undertaken. The trustees, with one exception, were chosen from the city, and were Alexander McLeod, Samuel H. McKee, George Whittaker, William Nesbit, Henry Hennigar, Robert Chestnut, Robert Robertson, Gilbert T. Ray, John B. Gaynor, George A. Lockhart, James Bustin, John Owens, and Francis Jordan; Mr. Gaynor being chapel steward. The frame was given by Mr. Owens and the work progressed. The chapel was dedicated on June 7th, 1829, and was the first church built in Portland. The sermon in the morning was by Rev. Mr. Williams, from Isaiah, lx., 7, "And I will glorify the house of my glory." In the afternoon Rev. Mr. Pickles preached from Haggai, ii., 19, "This day I will bless you," and in the evening Rev. Mr. Strong, superintendent of the circuit, from 1 Corinthians, ii., 2, "For I determined not to know any thing among you, save Jesus Christ and him crucified." The church was seventy-nine feet long and fifty-three feet wide, having at first an end gallery, which was afterwards extended along each side resting on columns which were continued to the ceiling to support the roof. It cost £2,000, and when completed there was a large debt upon it. Some liberal subscriptions were made which, with the sale of preference pews, amounted to upwards of £700. On the 26th August, 1841, this church was burned, and as there was but £600 insurance upon it the loss was great. On the 30th August a meeting was held in the Germain street chapel to consider the advisability of rebuilding, when it was decided to proceed at once with the erection of a brick or stone building. The attendance was cheering, which was said to show the religious advantage of "the family compact." The meeting was opened by Rev. William Temple. The scriptural selection was that in reference to the proclamation of Cyrus as to the rebuilding of the temple, as found in

Ezra, i. and part of ii. The meeting continued with unabated interest till near eleven o'clock, when it was announced that the subscriptions amounted to £1,145 5s. The new church was opened on June 5th, 1842, sermons being preached by Rev. Messrs. Miller, Hennigar and Bamford. This church was considered a beautiful structure, neat and convenient, finished in excellent taste throughout, and was superior to the one destroyed. The school-room in the basement was almost entirely above ground. To the liberality as well as to the constant and judicious supervision of Mr. Owens the congregation was, as in the first instance, greatly indebted.

CARLETON.

Beginning with 1810 the Methodist ministers for thirty years visited Carleton with varied success. During the latter portion of that period they worshipped in what was known as the "free meeting house." The system of one house being held by different denominations, in this as well as in many other instances, was proved not to be a good one. Our people began to look about for a suitable site. Thomas Coram, Esq., generously offered two lots for the purpose, but they were thought not to be sufficiently central. At length, through the exertions of Alderman Salter, the corporation granted a freehold title to the property on Guildford street, one hundred feet square, and upon this site the building, in which worship has been conducted ever since, was built. The corner stone was laid by Isaac Olive, Esq., on Thursday, the 12th November, 1840. In the evening Rev. S. D. Rice, who was the minister in charge, preached from Isaiah, xxviii., 16, "Behold, I lay in Zion for a foundation a stone, a tried stone, a precious corner stone; a sure foundation." The circuits were then called,—Saint John (south), Saint John (north), and Carleton and Long Reach.

Coming back to Mr. Alder's time, a reference to the files of the Saint John *Courier* will disclose the exercises followed at the examination of the Sunday school. The item, under date December 20th, 1823, is as follows : "The examination of the Sunday school that assembles in the Methodist chapel occupied two mornings. The members of the committee and others who took part in the examination expressed their high approbation of the manner in which the different classes read, recited and answered their biblical questions. Bibles, Testaments and smaller works of a religious nature were bestowed upon many as rewards for their diligence and good conduct." In the same paper, under date 15th December, 1824, is the the statement : " In 1822 an association called the Saint John Female Wesleyan Missionary Association was formed for the purpose of aiding, by penny-a-week subscriptions, the funds of the Wesleyan Missionary Society, and the collectors since that period raised upwards of £80."

On Monday, 19th September, 1825, the centenary of Mr. Wesley's ordination was celebrated. A discourse on the origin, nature, progress and present state of Methodism was delivered in the evening by the resident missionary, Mr. Alder.

In October, 1833, the chapel, after having been enlarged so as to give additional sittings to upwards of two hundred persons, was re-opened. Interesting services were held by Mr. Busby, the missionary in charge, and Rev. Mr. Wood, who at this time was stationed in Fredericton. Before leaving this division it may be interesting to note the names of some of the local preachers who at this time and for some time after were engaged in active work as such.

In 1834, from a plan of preaching places, it would appear that services were held in the City chapel, Portland, Carleton, Lower Cove, Alms House, Gondola Point, Mispeck and Loch Lomond. The ministers on the circuit were Rev. S. Busby and Rev. Mr. Smithson. They were ably assisted by a band of worthy local preachers, among whom were William Till, S. Hanford McKee, Mathew Thomas, William Nesbit, Thomas Furness, and perhaps some others. Mr. Till was the senior local preacher; was a native of New Brunswick, and converted early in life under the preaching of Joshua Marsden. In stature he was tall; in aspect modest. Mr. Daniel says of him : "He was a Christian to look at." He was sensible, though somewhat slow in speech and movement, but always commanded an attentive hearing. At an early period in his Christian experience he felt a strong call to the ministry, but allowed himself to be dissuaded. He consistently followed and faithfully labored in his Master's work until his death, which occurred in 1862. His connection with the first Sabbath school in Saint John has already been noted. In 1836 Mr. Till assumed control of the *City Gazette* and published it until 1840, and during the same years issued the *Christian Reporter and Temperance Advocate*. After relinquishing newspaper work he became a clerk, and for many years was employed in Tisdale's hardware store.

Samuel Hanford McKee was an earnest, active, old-time Methodist. He kept a house of entertainment on the Market square, where Messrs. Daniel & Boyd now do business. He was much respected by all with whom he had dealings. As a local preacher he was acceptable, and, no doubt, by his uprightness of conduct and piety of life as well as by his pulpit efforts, he exercised an influence for good on the community in which for so long a time he lived. He died June 26, 1835, aged sixty-two.

Mathew Thomas was an interesting exhorter; as a local preacher perhaps his ability was not of as high an order as that of some others with whom he was associated; nevertheless he did a great deal of good work in that line, and was employed as a hired local preacher, laboring in different localities, notably Grand Lake. It was his pride to proclaim himself a Methodist.

William Nesbit, a native of Berwickshire, Scotland, was a very superior and useful man; his talents were of a high order. In addition to taking his appointments as local preacher he was frequently called upon to take part at missionary meetings and watch-night services. On the 13th August, 1841, he passed to his reward, aged sixty-nine years, having been a Methodist forty years.

Not less active or useful, and perhaps more frequently called upon, was Thomas Hutchings, a gentleman whom many Varley school boys will remember with pleasure. Mr. Hutchings was born September 12, 1804, at Falmouth, England, and died November 5, 1856, triumphing in faith of the Gospel. He was converted early in life and when about twenty-one years of age became a class leader and local preacher, the duties of which office he efficiently discharged for more than thirty years. His widow, at a very advanced age, still survives, and his children, influenced by noble example and pious training, are all living useful lives and engaged in active Christian work.

From time to time the Germain street chapel was repaired and altered and came to be known as the mother of them all. It was one of the first buildings on the higher ground which yielded to the devastating demands of the great fire of 1877.

There are hallowed associations and sacred memories in connection with the old church that no material fire, be it ever so cruel and relentless, can destroy. In a new and grander building, on, perhaps, a more eligible site, the incense of praise is now offered, but until this generation shall pass away the old corner and its unpretentious, though comfortable old church, with its school-room and class-rooms, will be held very dear.

The title given to this work suggests its own divisions,—
Early Methodism : Centenary Church. In reference to the
first, perhaps enough has now been said ; the remaining pages
should be devoted to a consideration of the church whose
jubilee has suggested the preparation of this paper.

CENTENARY CHURCH.

After the enlargement of the Germain street church in
1833, and during the incumbency of Rev. Enoch Wood, who
was appointed to Saint John in 1836, the congregation became
too large for the building, the question of the erection of the
Centenary church was discussed. Formidable difficulties were
apparent, but a board of trustees was appointed and a site, in
what was then a most unpromising locality, was selected. Mr.
Wood was the leader in the enterprise, and by skilful management and indomitable perseverance, he and his co-laborers
succeeded in their work. Mr. Wood purchased three lots of
land for the Centenary trustees, paying $1,500 therefor. Mr.
John B. Gaynor paid $500 for a fourth, and gave the lot as a
donation for the purposes of the church. These four lots constituted the site on which Centenary church was subsequently
built. At three o'clock on Sunday, the 15th day of July, 1838,
Rev. Enoch Wood preached at an open air service held on the
floor of the chapel then being erected. An account of that
service and of the laying of the corner stone may be found in
the Saint John *Observer* of that time, and is as follows :

"Divine service was held on Sabbath afternoon last upon
the floor of the new Wesleyan chapel which is being erected
in Saint George's street in this city. The Rev. Enoch Wood
addressed a concourse of people in the open air, supposed to
amount to two thousand, from 1 Corinthians, 1st chap., 23rd
and 24th verses. This interesting exercise was concluded by

Messrs. Busby and McNutt. On Monday, at eleven o'clock, a large and respectable assembly convened at the same place to witness the ceremony usually observed by the Wesleyans in laying the corner or foundation stone of their houses for sacred worship. The service was begun by the Rev. Richard Sheppard, and the people addressed by the Rev. Messrs. Busby and Wood. In the stone was inserted various documents, etc., so guarded as to secure their preservation. The venerable John Ferguson, Esq., who has been a member of the Wesleyan society for forty-seven years, laid the corner stone in a most devout and impressive manner, giving before the conclusion of the ceremony an account of the first winter he spent in the country, during which not a single sermon was preached in the town, if a town it might then be called. The building will be sixty feet by ninety feet from a very chaste design by Mr. Cunningham; there will be a large school-room and vestry underneath the chapel, and a furnace for heating the building with hot air. Provision will be made for four hundred sittings to be free. Advantage will be taken of the most modern improvements in finishing the interior so as to secure ease and comfort with a strict regard for prudence and economy. The foundation sills and first floor are all ready to receive the frame, which is in such a state of forwardness that in a few days the raising of it will be commenced. The situation is a very suitable one, standing upon high ground and in a part of the city which is enlarging very fast. If proper attention be paid to the finishing of it, not only will it be creditable to the numerous body of Christians under whose immediate auspices and exertions it is advancing and a powerful auxiliary in the great cause of religion, but it will be an ornament to our flourishing city."

In the aperture in the stone were placed an almanac of that year and a copy of *The Christian Reporter and Temperance*

Advocate and *The Courier*, and a parchment upon which were the following particulars, written by Thomas Hutchings: "This corner stone of the second Wesleyan Methodist chapel, commenced in the city of Saint John, New Brunswick, was laid by J. Ferguson, Esq. (who has been at this time a member of the society forty-five years), on the 16th day of July, 1838, in the first year of the reign of Her Majesty Queen Victoria; Sir John Harvey, K.C.B., lieutenant governor of the province; Robert F. Hazen, Esq., mayor of the city; Rev. Edmund Grindrod, president of the British conference; Rev. Messrs. Dr. Bunting, John Beecham, Robert Alder and Elijah Hoole, secretaries for foreign missions; Rev. William Temple, chairman of the New Brunswick district; Rev. Enoch Wood, superintendent of the city circuit; Richard Shephard, of Portland, and Stephen Bamford, supernumerary. At the time this stone was laid Messrs. Ferguson, G. T. Ray, George Whittaker, George A. Lockhart and John B. Gaynor were trustees for the Wesleyan chapel Germain street; Messrs. J. E. McDonald, Richard Whiteside, David Collins, Edward T. Knowles, William Whiteside and Henry Whiteside the building committee for the present chapel. Members in society: City, 380; Portland, 108. In the province, 22 Wesleyan missionaries and 2,490 members. There were present upon this occasion the Rev. Sampson Busby, the oldest missionary in the district, and the Rev. Arthur McNutt, the first visiting missionary appointed by the Wesleyans to labor in New Brunswick."

Forty years later, after the building had fed the fury of the fire of 1877, and all that was inflammable had been consumed, this document was removed from the place in which it had been for all that time. Beyond a few creases that necessarily were made in depositing it in a contracted place, it was found to be in as good condition as when placed there on July 16th, 1838. The newspapers and almanac were in like condition.

The original plan was made by Mr. Cunningham, architect, and the specification for the frame, etc., was made by Mr. Mitchell, architect, assisted by Henry Hennigar, Esq., of Her Majesty's Royal Engineering Department. The excavations for the basement and foundations were made by Messrs. McGuirk and McDade. The contract for the frame, boarding the whole building, shingling the roof and finishing the dome, cupola and tower down to the eaves, was taken by Mr. W. B. Frost, who was to find all the materials necessary for the completion of his contract. Mr. Frost employed Mr. Samuel C. Bugbee and Mr. Stevenson to oversee and carry on the work. The rest of the work necessary to complete the church was done by day's work, under the superintendence of Mr. Bugbee. The foundation wall was built by Mr. David S. Marshall, and the plastering done by Mr. Thomas P. Williams. The cost of the church was as follows:

Materials	£689	9s.	3d.
Cartage, etc	81	5	2½
Labor	2,873	15	10½
Sundries	6	15	4
Benches and hot air	78	0	0
Work benches and poles	11	12	3
General accounts	433	3	8
	£4,174	1s.	7d.
Purchase of land, interest on notes, law expenses, etc., etc	611	19	5
	£4,786	1s.	0d.

Upwards of £800 were subscribed towards the liquidation of the debt before the church was opened. For some years after the opening of the church the debt seemed to remain at about the same amount, for in 1845 we find it to have been £3,950.

It is of interest to note that the pulpit, which seems to have been a beautiful piece of work, was paid for by a number of ladies of the congregation whose names and the amounts given by them are as follows:

Mrs. Lockhart	£10	0s.	0d.
Mrs. Miles	5	0	0
Mrs. McKee	10	0	0
Mrs. Wallace	5	0	0
Mrs. McDonald	10	0	0
Mrs. Knowles	10	14	6
	£50	14s.	6d.

The pulpit was of a wine glass shape and was distant some eight or ten feet from the choir gallery. The minister to reach his place ascended a spiral stairway, and would give the choir the needed information as to the hymns to be sung at the service, by handing the slip at the point of a stick of sufficient length to cover the distance. This was certainly the practice with some of the ministers.

On the night before the opening of the church the city was visited by a terrible conflagration, in which many business houses were destroyed, involving much distress. The losses with which our people met, occasioned by the fire and commercial depression incident thereto, prevented a more generous response than was given. Yet, through the persuasion of Dr. Wood, many amounts in small sums were given. Nor should we overlook the fact that there were some exceedingly generous gifts. Mrs. Nelles states that her father (Dr. Wood), would often talk of the time he had in collecting money to build Centenary church. One instance he seemed to enjoy and tell with great pleasure. He was soliciting a subscription from a lady and was refused. He replied to her, "Well, sister, when you worship in the church you will have the extreme happiness and satisfaction of knowing you have not given one cent towards a brick." She afterwards sent him a good subscription.

Dr. Wood,—whose name and memory are revered in this city among the older Methodists not only by reason of his personal worth, but also because of his associations with the inception and completion of this enterprise, and of his activity in advancing all matters of interest and importance to the church with which he was ministerially connected,—contributed an article to one of our missionary periodicals in reference to "Centenary church as it was." The contribution may very properly be reproduced, and is as follows :

"After spending two years of active missionary life in Miramichi, and three years on the Fredericton circuit, in 1836 I was re-appointed to the Saint John circuit, having for my fellow-laborer the genial and devoted minister of Christ, the Rev. Arthur McNutt. He had spent a year with me as a single man and a member of my family on the Miramichi mission; it was a great pleasure to both of us to renew our brotherly associations in our common Master's vineyard. We found in Saint John a loving and united people and good congregations in the Germain street church. The only other sanctuary we had at that time was in Portland, where the Protestant population was thin and the society feeble. That in Germain street was forty by eighty, and the ground at the end of it had recently been filled up by the erection of a two-story building, the lower part of which formed a commodious and convenient vestibule, with a large room for prayer and class meetings; the upper part had a concave ceiling and made a fine school room eighty feet long. Adjoining the church on

Germain street was the parsonage, or, as it was then called, the mission house, to which a story was added after I assumed the superintendency and the whole put into excellent repair at a cost of £400 currency. Before the end of the first year it became apparent, if we were faithful to our calling, we should be preparing for the erection of another sanctuary. The pressure for accommodation had become so great that many families had to divide in their attendance, some coming in the morning of each Sabbath and some in the evening. For some time it seemed to me paradoxical to hear men most devoutly pray for the enlargement of the church in its membership by the conversion of sinners when they had not a pew to place them in without thrusting others aside. So deep were our convictions of duty that we could no longer remain inactive, and believing in the call of God to 'arise and build,' and relying upon the benevolence and sympathy of His people, together with the favorable tendency of the public mind, three lots were purchased from the Messrs. Sears for $500 each. Plans were obtained; a board of new trustees was formed, and without a dollar in the chest the erection of the church was begun. The lots of land on which the building was to be placed presented formidable obstacles to rapid advancement. In the centre the pointed crags were about twelve feet above the level of the street, and the basement being intended to be eleven feet in the clear, hundreds of cart loads were removed in making the excavation for the foundation walls. In size the building was sixty feet by ninety feet, of which the accompanying sketch gives a tolerably good idea of its external expression though failing to convey a correct view of the small columns, mouldings, etc., which ornamented the entrances and other portions of the sacred structure, put up with Sir Christopher Wren's judgment, in view of the beauty of proportions,— one-third less in width as related to length. When completed in 1839 it was dedicated to the service of Almighty God by the Rev. Dr. Alder, then one of the missionary secretaries of the parent society, and the Rev. Dr. Richey, both distinguished for their commanding oratory.

"Its erection was embarrassed by two terrible conflagrations, which greatly deranged the business community, and especially affected many of those who had most at heart the success of this godly enterprise. The first money paid on account of the projected church was by Brother John B. Gaynor, who put down on the superintendent's study table ten five pound notes of the Bank of New Brunswick. He then generously stated that it was his intention to purchase and present to the church the fourth lot which constituted the block, eighty feet by two hundred feet, whenever it was in the market; this he faithfully carried out at a cost of £150. The next largest sum on the list was £100 by the late Gilbert T. Ray. Our people were not wealthy, but they all gave of their substance willingly; nor were we wanting in many expressions of good-will, in the form of help from other denominations. In 1846 the committee in London having promised £500 sterling, on condition the same amount should be raised in Saint John, to remove the existing debt, a public meeting of the Wesleyans was called and the amount promptly contributed.

"In the course of years God greatly honored his servants appointed to labor there; it was indeed 'His rest,'—His 'dwelling place.' One of the most extensive revivals ever known in the province was conducted in the Centenary by the late Rev. Dr. Knight and the brethren associated with him. Of this holy house it may be truly said:

> "And in the great decisive day,
> When God the nations shall survey,
> *It shall* before the world appear
> That crowds were born to glory *there*

"That the new Centenary 'and the mother of them all,' old Germain street church, may surpass their predecessors in durability of material, architectural beauty, and above all in greater numbers of spiritual worshippers within their sacred walls is a prayer in which thousands will join with

"ENOCH WOOD.

"Mission Rooms, Toronto, August 6th, 1878."

A letter from Mr. Smallwood, who was the first pastor of Centenary congregation, dated Charlottetown, P. E. I., February 12th, 1889, bearing upon this subject would also be of interest:

"Your letter was duly received and contents noted; but though the first put in charge of the Centenary church after it was opened, yet that date was so anterior to the present, many things have slipped from my memory during the roll of nearly fifty years, but I do remember that on the Saturday night before the opening of said church, which was on the Sunday, we were engaged in holding a centenary meeting in the old Germain street, when the fire-bell rang out the alarm of fire. The congregation at once scattered and the ministers were left alone on the platform,—Dr. Robert Alder, the chairmain, being in the midst of us. That night portions of Prince William street and Market square were licked up by the fire fiend. The opening Sunday was a sorrowful day in Saint John, but Dr. Alder and Dr. Richey, the one from London and the other from Coburg, proceeded with the opening services and their sermons were worthy of the occasion.

"I then took charge and preached on the following Sunday. The congregation was small, but the increase was marvelous, for in less than a year the church was as well filled as I ever saw it in after years. The Rev. Richard Williams was my superintendent; he lived in the Germain street mission house.

Rev. Enoch Wood was in Portland, and I as a probationer, though ordained in England, resided with William Whiteside in Elliott Row. Week night services for both prayer and preaching were at once established; several class meetings started; sacraments duly administered, and a revival blessed us towards the end of the year. At this period Mr. Williams left the circuit and with his family went to England, and the Rev. William Temple assumed the office of superintendent. Rev. S. Rice was brought to the city with especial regard to the necessities of the infant Methodist cause in Carleton. Brother Rice got the church built in Carleton during that year, but he resided nevertheless in Saint John and boarded with Mr. James McDonald on Princess street. During this, my second year at the Centenary church, Dr. Pickard, S. D. Rice, and, I think, Samuel McMasters were set apart by ordination to the work of the ministry. The service was held in the Centenary church. The building was crowded, and the galleries being free they were crowded to excess. It was one of the most interesting services which I ever attended. During that year a wonderful revival set in and over two hundred added to the company of believers.

"The church was built principally through the agency of the late Dr. Wood. It was in the wind that measures were being taken in view of that result. When an outsider asked a Methodist on the street if such was the case, the answer was in the affirmative; but said the other, 'Have the Methodists *said really* that they *will* build a £5,000 church among those nigger huts and slaughter houses?' The reply was, 'Yes, they have.' 'Well,' said the other, 'If they have said they will, *it will be done;* there is no doubt of that.' But the day it was opened there was a debt upon it nearly equal to the whole of the outlay. Unfriendly eyes looked on expecting that it would be sold by auction to meet the expense of its erection, and that they would slip in and purchase it as a house in which to promulge another creed ; but it went on to completion and the noble Methodists of Saint John, with the trustees of the premises, toiled to keep down the debt, and amid a world of discouragements, it has continued a Methodist church to this day. "I am, yours truly, "F. SMALLWOOD."

In the year 1839 the centennial of Methodism was observed throughout the connection by religious services and the presentation of thank offerings. It was expected that perhaps seventy or eighty thousand pounds would be raised. The whole Methodist world, however, responded to the call, with the result that the celebration was such as had never been equalled by any Protestant denomination either in its magnificence or its liberality. The aggregate sum contributed by the various Methodist bodies in England and America was more than seventeen hundred thousand dollars, without interfering with stated collections ; and in a year of unparalled commercial depression. The name given to the new church in Saint John and by which it has since been known was suggested by this memorable event.

The church was opened on the 18th day of August, by special dedicatory services conducted in the morning and evening by Rev. Mathew Richey and Rev. Robert Alder respectively. Rev. William Croscombe was advertized to preach in the afternoon, but there is no record of his having done so, and the belief is that he was not present.

Dr. Richey was a native of the north of Ireland and came to Saint John at an early age. At sixteen he began to preach in this city and must have been received on trial in connecction with the British conference at about the age of twenty. He labored in Nova Scotia on several circuits, and in 1835 we find him in Montreal and later in Toronto ; and in 1839 he was at Coburg as principal of the Upper Canada Academy,

CENTENARY CHURCH AT TIME OF OPENING.

now Victoria College. It was while he was in this relation that he visited Saint John and preached the opening sermon in old Centenary. He is described as at that time about thirty-four years of age, very tall and slender, but straight and graceful, as were all his movements. His hair was very light colored and very curly, surmounting what an American writer pronounced "a comely old country face." For the power and pleasantness of his voice; ease and gracefulness of elocution; ready command of the most exuberant and elevated language, amounting almost to inflation of style; together with a rich variety of theological lore, he scarcely ever had a superior, if an equal, in British North America. He was gentlemanlike in his manner, Christian in his spirit and demeanor and soundly Wesleyan in his teachings.*

He was of fine presence; voice so full, deep and musical, that it might well be said to be phenomenal; faultless as a reader, it was a rare treat to hear him read the Word of God. His pulpit efforts were marked by a solemn and devotional spirit; his prayers were in striking contrast to that hasty, irreverent manner which characterizes the approaches of so many, in our day, to the throne of grace. †

His sermon at the dedication was based upon Ephesians, iii., 8-10. The subject being "the exalted objects of the Christian ministry." It may be found in Volume I. of *British North American Wesleyan Methodist Magazine,* or in the volume of his published sermons under the title indicated. His concluding words were: "Whenever I pass the threshold of the sanctuary, I feel that I stand on sacred ground; there 'awful voices' are heard, and holy inspirations breathe; before

---

*Case and his Contemporaries, iv., 108.

† "British Wesleyanism in Toronto." Senator McDonald in *Methodist Magazine*

me stands a man of like passions with myself,—but though no halo of celestial radiance encircle his brow, nor demonstrations of omnipotence attest his mission, not the less do I recognize in him a minister from no earthly court,—a commissioned *ambassador of Christ.*

> " 'There stands
> The legate of the skies! His theme divine,
> His office sacred, his credentials clear.
> By him the violated law speaks out
> Its thunders, and by him, in strains as sweet
> As angels use, the Gospel whispers peace.'

"O what must be the moral grandeur of His theme; what the importance of the destiny that hangs on the reception of His message; since the one challenges and rewards the profoundest investigation, while the other wakes the deepest sympathies of 'the principalities and powers in heavenly places!'

"Men and brethren! I have but a single question to propose in conclusion, and if while the *unsearchable riches of Christ* have been displayed you have not listened with the ear of the sceptical or the careless, I unsolicitously commit its solution and its practical operation to your own hearts and consciences, HOW SHALL WE ESCAPE IF WE NEGLECT SO GREAT SALVATION?"

Rev. Robert Alder had recently arrived from England. Soon after his arrival the degree of D. D. was conferred upon him by Middletown University. Advantage was taken by our people of his presence in this country, not only because of the distinguished position he held, coming from England officially, and of his pulpit eminence, but also in recognition of his valuable services and popular pastorates already mentioned.

The church thus dedicated was not in a field in which a

congregation had been gradually gathered prior to its erection, but was one for which the people waited; the people who had said, as said the sons of the prophets unto Elisha, "Behold now, the place where we dwell with thee, is too strait for us. Let us go we pray thee *   *   and take thence every man a beam, and let us make us a place, where we may dwell."

The services in the old church were omitted for that day, and though there were the gloom and depression throughout the city that are incident to such calamities as that of the preceding night, yet the congregations at the opening services were large and attentive. The congregational singing, led by the united choirs, was hearty; the services altogether deeply interesting, and it was felt to be a great day for Methodism in Saint John.

The collections at the opening services amounted to £52 4s. 1d. After the dedication, church organization was effected, and Robert Bennison, a leading musician of the day, became leader of the choir. Some persons assert that the first leader was James E. McDonald. Whether Mr. McDonald was or not it is certain that he was a prominent member and beyond doubt led the singing at the social services in the earlier years. Of the original choir not many now survive. Mr. John J. Munroe, of this city, was a member. So were Mr. and Mrs. Broderick, who now live at Jacksonville in Carleton county. Mr. Broderick is over eighty years of age and has not been in the city during the last forty years.

The second leader was Mr. J. N. C. Black, who was at that time a North wharf merchant. He took a deep interest in the choir and spent a large sum of money in maintaining it. There was no instrumental accompaniment, but Mr. Black used a bass-viol, with which he started the tunes.

Mr. Broderick became the third leader. Messrs. Samuel and James Bustin and Thomas Brundage were among the singers, while some of the female singers were Mrs. Broderick, Miss McAdam (Mrs. Samuel Jordan), Miss Letitia Lowery, Miss Susan Hennigar (Mrs. McCarty), Miss Gove (Mrs. D. H. Hall), Mrs. McLaughlin, Miss Jones (Mrs. James Robertson).

Mr. James Bustin was the next leader. He would catch the note and set the tune by means of a sounding fork. The male singers then were Samuel Bustin, George Bustin, Jacob V. Troop and Gilbert Bent. The female singers were the Misses McKillop (Mrs. James and Mrs. Charles Bustin), Miss Margaret Smith (Mrs. Parks, who joined the upper choir years ago), Miss Charlotte Smith (Mrs. Venning), Misses Lizzie and Jane Sancton (Mrs. Whittaker and Mrs. Brown), Miss Julia Bustin, Miss Jane Reid (Mrs. Spurr of Liverpool), Miss Mary Jane McLean (Mrs. Nisbett), Miss Janey Eaton (Mrs. Smith), and Miss Lizzie Lawton (Mrs. Ennis). This must have been the choir somewhere about 1851 and up to 1853.

The week night services in Centenary were held on Monday and Thursday, and in Germain street on Tuesday and Friday. On Wednesday evening a service known as the Collins' prayer meeting was held, at first in David Collins' house on Horsfield street, and later, when more accommodation was required, in the vestry of Germain street. This prayer meeting was one of great power and blessing,—continual conversions were the result of it, and from it the membership of the church was largely increased. It was certainly unique in its national representation. Mr. Collins, the leader, was from the north of Ireland; Isaac Johnston and wife from Yorkshire, with most pronounced accent; James Clerio from Scotland; Mrs. Thomas, known as Aunt Ann Thomas, also from Scotland; John Anderson, a Dane, speaking very imperfect English; Mr. and Mrs. Oates from the Isle of Man, besides many others, were members. Messrs. James and Dennis Sullivan, who arrived in this country in 1837, joined this prayer meeting. The latter brethren came from Bandon, Ireland, about twenty miles from Cork. Thus, besides natives, there were English, Irish, Scotch, Danish and Manx people.

The first revival of religion, after the opening of Centenary, may be said to have begun on September 11th, 1840, though there had been expectancy for some months before that day. On the day mentioned, after the customary evening service, those under conviction were invited to kneel around the communion rail, and ten persons, who had resisted all former appeals, singled themselves out for mercy. Thus encouraged, prayer meetings were appointed for six o'clock in the morning of each day, which were well attended; a fast day was appointed and on that day three meetings were held. During the week between twenty and thirty conversions were reported. The young men held a weekly meeting at a distant part of the city. Sabbath school teachers were very active in their classes and the good work soon was manifest in the schools. Beginning with the boys it soon extended to the girls. Select classes were formed and suitable leaders appointed. The quarterly fast, which is said to have been a brook by the way, was held on 2nd October. Centenary school-room not being completed, the vestry of Germain street church became the place of meeting, but was entirely too small for the number of people who assembled. The Sabbath congregations increased wonderfully and the revival went on, lasting about two years. In this the churches united of course, as they did in every special work for many years.

In early Methodist days hymn books were scarce, and the average memory perhaps could not retain a whole verse of the hymn being sung. The ministers accommodated the people by only reading two lines at a time. So rigid was the custom that punctuation marks had no influence whatever. This practice prevailed in Centenary church for some time after the opening. Possibly, years hence the present custom of lining out hymns may be considered quite as absurd.

Love-feasts were regularly held for years; in fact such regularity has only been broken into of late. These services were exceedingly profitable. At first they were union services, but it was not long before each church held its own. One sometimes hears the remark, "that it is a pity that the love-feast with which our fathers were familiar is so rare a feature in modern Methodism." It is not because they are no longer part of the Methodist discipline that they are not observed.

Quarterly fasts were fixed by rule for the first Friday after Lady-day, Midsummer-day, Michaelmas-day and Christmas-day.

For many years a very profitable and well attended seven o'clock prayer meeting was held on Sunday morning.

The watch-night service in its origin, of course, is purely Methodistic. These services have been held in Saint John probably without a break ever since the introduction of Methodism therein. They began at an earlier hour and lasted later than is the custom at present, and were held in each church.

The renewal of the covenant was a united service, and usually held in Centenary church on New Year's day. Admission to it, as well as to love-feasts, involved the production of a society ticket.

Services were held on Good Friday as now, but on Christmas day there were morning and evening services.

The hours of service on Sabbath were eleven and six. The evening service was usually followed by a prayer meeting.

Of the prayer meetings, Mr. Peter Le Sueur, an early official and active member of Centenary, but now resident in Ottawa, says: "They were among the most profitable services I ever attended, and I think of them after the lapse of over forty years with grateful feelings."

Mr. Cooney, of a later period, in his autobiography, says: "Of all the prayer meetings held throughout this great continent among Wesleyans or any other denomination of Christians, perhaps there is not one better attended, or one that is more distinguished for devotional fervour and divine unction than the Monday evening prayer meeting held in the basement story of the Centenary chapel in the city of Saint John. There are few circuits, if any, within the same vast extent, favored with a more efficient staff of 'praying brethren.' In this spirited band David Collins, Henry Marshall, Edward Lloyd and others occupy a distinguished place."

Candles were still largely used for the purpose of light, but the chief illumination in the new church came from a magnificent chandelier, which was decorated with prismy pendants, and, as an ornament, was said to have been the most beautiful thing of that line in the city. Thirty-six lamps filled with porpoise oil placed in this chandelier, caused great strain to the chain or rope sustaining it, which was only equal to the demand made upon it down to the year 1842. In that year it broke and the beautiful chandelier, of which the congregation were so proud, became a complete wreck. In its fall the sexton narrowly escaped serious injury.

FIRST MISSIONARY MEETING.

On Thursday, the 11th February, 1841, the first missionary meeting was held in the church, the speakers being Messrs. Temple, Bamford, Busby, Leggett, Smallwood and Rice. An account of this meeting, as published at the time, is as follows: "A little before seven o'clock the fine-toned bell, weighing 1,524 pounds, recently erected in the tower, gave loud intimation of the approaching exercises; that spacious and handsome edifice was filled by an immense assembly, who manifested the deepest interest in the proceedings. This was the first missionary meeting held in this chapel (itself the fruit of missionary labors and success), at which G. T. Ray, Esq., was called to preside; his address commenced by an expression of the honor conferred upon him in thus being invited to conduct the first and so large and respectable a meeting as that before him; and among other things he referred to the authority under which missionary exertions were made. The several speakers before enumerated earnestly pleaded the cause of the perishing heathen, and never did they succeed better or more to the delight and satisfaction of an audience. Like Elihu, they seemed 'full of matter, and the spirit within constrained them.' To God be all the glory! A society was organized in connection with this chapel, whose gatherings we anticipate will greatly swell the missionary income of the circuit. Collections, £32 5s. 0d."

Mr. John Ferguson, of whom mention has been made as having laid the corner stone, was not at this meeting, having departed this life nine days previous thereto. The deceased was a native of Armagh, Ireland; born in February, 1757; entered the army when but young, and secured his discharge in 1804. He came to Saint John in 1789, and was pay-sergeant in the second battalion of the Royal Artillery. In 1792 he joined the Wesleyan society under the ministry of Rev. James Mann. To his intelligence, zeal and liberality our cause in this city was at all times indebted. Through his exertions the Germain street chapel was begun and completed,—he having undertaken the responsibility of the debt. He was a trustee of that chapel; a leader in the society, and for many years a teacher in the Sunday school,—and as already stated, laid the corner stone of the new church. In the enjoyment of that peace which "passeth all understanding," he, without pain and in the strongest assurance of a joyful resurrection unto eternal life, quietly fell asleep in Jesus on the 2nd February, 1841, in the eighty-fourth year of his age. His grave is but a few steps from that of Mr. Bamford in the Methodist burial ground of this city, neglected and overgrown. On a tomb-table over his grave the statement may with difficulty now be read, "that during a long life he maintained a most unblemished reputation for the development of principles of the strictest integrity, while his ardent and growing piety rendered him a blessing to the community and an useful and active member of the church of Christ."

FIRST TEA MEETING.

A tea meeting in those days seems to have been regarded almost as a means of grace. In support of the statement an article, under the head of "Religious Intelligence," from the *British North American Wesleyan Magazine* for 1842, giving an account of a tea meeting held in the latter part of November, 1841, is reproduced. It is given the more readily because of the claims made for this particular entertainment: "To extend the cause of piety and place the church in a position of freedom and usefulness is a subject worthy of the highest thoughts of man. In the absence of endowed resources ingenious methods have been devised to create or augment supplies, so necessary to carry out zealous plans for the diffusion of religious knowledge, in which the spiritual welfare of hundreds of immortal souls is involved. As colonists we are emulous to follow good examples set us by the churches in the mother country, and especially when our social enjoyments can be rendered so tributary to the interests of Zion, while at the same time we are maintaining and improving our religious character. Thousands of pounds sterling are annually raised for extending the boundaries of the Redeemer's kingdom; towards this as an efficient auxiliary may be enumerated breakfast and tea meetings. Scarcely a file of papers falls into our hands, connected with any of the leading denominations in England, but in them are found accounts of these meetings. It has long been thought that the practice might be introduced here with great advantage, and we rejoice to be enabled to place on record an account of the *first* which has been held in the New Brunswick District,—perhaps the first ever held in British North America.

"Preparations were made by excavating the rock under the Centenary chapel, in St. George's street, for a commodious school-room, vestry and class-rooms. When the chapel was opened these remained unfinished for a year-and-a-half before any effort was made to bring them into use. In the winter of 1840-41 the subject was brought before the notice of the teachers of the Sunday school which had been organized in the gallery of the chapel ; the female teachers succeeded in raising upwards of £60, with which a commencement was made to finish the rooms. Before this was done the expenditure had gone considerably beyond our resources ; to provide for this the suggestion was made that we might succeed by a voluntary tea meeting. About forty ladies of the several Wesleyan congregations agreed cheerfully to provide each a table for twelve guests; some entered so heartily into the plan that they provided two tables. It was agreed that the fare should be simple ; that this part of our social enjoyment might be rendered tributary to the higher intellectual and spiritual exercises of the evening.

"At least 500 persons were in the room, all of whom wore expressions upon their countenances of universal delight. Two suitable Psalms were read and the usual poetic grace sung :

>   " 'Be present at our table Lord,
>   Be here and everywhere ador'd ;
>   Thy creatures bless, and grant that we
>   May feast in paradise with thee.'

"The repast concluded, all heartily joined in expressions of gratitude by singing :

    " 'We thank thee, Lord, for this our food,
    But more because of Jesus' blood ;
    Let manna to our souls be given,
    Sent from the tree of life in heaven.'

"The Rev. Mr. Temple presided over the meeting, and gave an animated address upon the importance and advantage of early religious education. Prayer was then made by the Rev. E. Wood, for the blessing of God to rest upon the exertions which would be made there to impart the knowledge of Christ to hundreds of youth. This part of the service evidently was attended with a gracious feeling, which increased with the address of each succeeding speaker. Messrs. Robinson and Beckwith, the two Baptist ministers stationed in the city, both addressed the meeting with good effect ; the other speakers were Messrs. Wood, Rice and Pickard. In consequence of the last disastrous fire we had to postpone the meeting a week, and thereby lost the valuable services of our brethren,— Bamford, of Digby ; Pickles, of Sheffield, and Barret, of Sussex Vale,—all of whom had kindly made their way to Saint John to share in the duties and pleasures of these opening services, but whose engagements would not admit of their remaining the whole of another week. After paying what expenses were incurred, more than £50 were passed to the credit of the trust-fund."

The exact amount was £51 7s. 6d. This, then, was the beginning of tea meetings in New Brunswick and possibly in British North America. The temperance soiree held in the school-room of the Germain street chapel in 1838, on the occasion of the Queen's coronation, not being in the nature of a tea meeting, in no way interferes with the claims urged for this gathering.

Mr. Le Sueur, in his letter already quoted from, says: "Among the very enjoyable things in the Centenary were the tea meetings, where there was perhaps over-much rivalry to furnish the tables; but that aside, the re-unions were singularly pleasant and conducive to social intercourse." During the fifty years a vast amount of money has been raised by tea meetings and other methods of like character. Not only have the trust funds been thus augmented, but the people look back upon the occasions with very pleasant recollections.

The returns made to the district meeting in 1840 showed that there were 351 members of the society in Saint John South. In 1842 the number returned was 458, with sixty-one on trial, an increase of nearly one-third. In the report is the statement that, "Of those on trial the most are children from nine to seventeen years of age; but their walk is worthy the gospel. The young brethren, Messrs. Smallwood and Rice, have labored indefatigably during the year, and, it is only due to them to say, that the revival of which we have been a witness was owing instrumentally to them."

In 1841 Rev. S. D. Rice was appointed to the circuit in Mr. Smallwood's place, and Mr. Temple entered upon his second year as superintendent. Rev. H. Pickard was also appointed to Saint John South for that year, more especially that he might edit and conduct a monthly publication known as the *British North American Wesleyan Magazine*. This magazine was continued for five years, and for the most of that period was conducted by Rev. William Temple, he having succeeded Mr. Pickard. It was discontinued in deference to the wishes of the home conference,—that body fearing that the interests of the *Wesleyan Methodist Magazine* were prejudiced by its publication. The action of the conference was felt to be ill-timed as the magazine was ably conducted and much appreciated. For the time being it was the repository of much that was then profitable reading, and is now valuable as historical data. In the next year, 1842, the appointments were Rev. William Temple superintendent, Rev. E. Wood and Rev. W. Allen; Messrs. Rice and Pickard being removed. Centenary was peculiarly Mr. Wood's charge, and Mr. Temple, in addition to his other duties, assumed the editorship of the magazine. Mr. Wood remained for four years, being superintendent for the last three.

The ordination service, to which Mr. Smallwood refers, seems to have been of a most interesting character. It was held on Monday evening, the 30th May, 1842. The night was exceedingly unfavorable, nevertheless the building was crowded to excess. The brethren ordained to the ministry were Messrs. S. D. Rice, H. Pickard and S. McMasters. An appropriate charge was given by Rev. S. Busby and an interesting address delivered to the congregation by Rev. S. Bamford. Dr. Pickard, in March, 1889, in referring to this service, says: "The fact which I am led to notice, that all the ministers who took part in the solemn ceremony, as well as the two brethren who were ordained with me, have finished their life's work, is to my mind a very impressive one. My ordination papers are signed, W. Temple, chairman; Enoch Wood, secretary; James G. Hennigar, Albert DesBrisay, Richard Shepherd." It is needless to say that Messrs. Rice and Pickard, during a long ministry, were most useful members of the conferences to which they were attached, and every forward movement of our church has been influenced by reason of the enlightened judgment they have brought to bear upon it. Mr. McMasters, at the time of his ordination, was said to be the picture of health, possessing what was termed an iron constitution, and seemed to have the promise of a long and useful ministry, while his companions were considered to be far from robust; but "the race is not always to the swift, nor the battle to the strong." On the 21st of the following

September he was taken sick at Fredericton, and, against the wishes of his friends, determined to hurry to his residence on the Nashwaak, where, on the fourth of October, he died. A few hours before his death, he said to Mr. Busby: "The love of God to me is inexpressible; it is like the rain coming down from heaven to my soul." Funeral sermons were preached on the following Sabbath,—in the morning at Nashwaak by the Rev. H. Pickard, and in the evening at Fredericton by the Rev. S. D. Rice, his companions at the ordination.

The year 1843 was remarkable for the great number of removals, caused by the commercial depression in the city. The return to the district for that year is: "While through the derangements in the mercantile community several thousand have left the city, we report with thankfulness that our congregations were never so steady or large as they are at the present time."

There were now two Methodist chapels, but the relation they occupied to the circuit needs explanation. The ministers, one of whom was superintendent, were appointed, generally, to the circuit known as Saint John South, and neither of them to a particular church in that circuit. The affairs of both churches were administered by one quarterly board, though each had its trustee board. This state of things existed until 1867; but from the first it seemed well understood that when a minister came to the circuit he would immediately enter upon pastoral relations with a particular church, and in that way Mr. Smallwood, for instance, in his letter on page 52, speaks of himself as being "the first put in charge of Centenary church."

The earliest existing minutes of the Centenary trustees are those of a meeting held on 29th January, 1841. At this meeting Rev. Mr. Temple presided. The minutes are partly in his hand-writing. There were also present Messrs. J. E. Mc-

Donald, E. T. Knowles, W. Whiteside and Richard Whiteside. The only business transacted was the opening and consideration of tenders, of which there were six, handed in for completion of the basement so far as the joiner work was concerned. Mr. Samuel Bugbee's being the lowest, the figures being £50, was accepted.

The next meeting of which there is a record was held on February 2nd, 1845, and from that time to the present all minutes have been duly recorded in books kept for that purpose. At this meeting Mr. Wood presided. The trustees present were Messrs. R. Whiteside, E. T. Knowles, G. T. Ray and Henry Whiteside; while Messrs. A. Eaton, John Gardner, James Smith, Richard W. Thorne and P. LeSueur were present as friends, by invitation. The chairman stated that in consequence of the continued absence of one of the trustees and the separation of others from the society, the number was reduced to five, and that the separation of one more would prevent the remaining four from performing any acts requiring legal precision. He thought it desirable to increase the number to twelve or fifteen. He intimated that the course contemplated by the then trustees was first to make a strenuous effort to raise not less than ONE THOUSAND POUNDS, which, if successful, would enable him to draw for a grant of £500 from the London committee,—conditionally made in aid of the chapel fund. The friends present were affectionately requested to assist in the intended effort and to accept the responsibility of trustees. Messrs. Eaton, Gardner and Smith declined the trusteeship, but expressed their willingness heartily to co-operate in the endeavor to raise the required amount. Messrs. Thorne and Le Sueur consented to act and were appointed to office. At this meeting Mr. Le Sueur was appointed chapel steward, which office he held from that time until his removal from the city in May, 1849. At the next meeting Mr. Henry Marshall was asked to assist the steward, and having consented he faithfully attended to his duties for many years. A letter from the London committee was read, setting forth that in consideration of the calamitous fires which had occurred in Saint John, as well as of other adverse events, through the influence of which the Centenary chapel had been kept in pecuniary embarassment, and also as a proof of their anxiety of the spiritual welfare of the society, they offered to give a sum of five hundred pounds sterling towards the liquidation of the debt,—providing a further sum of one thousand pounds was raised for the same object in Saint John. Whereupon it was resolved, "That the communication, as made by Mr. Wood, be received with heartfelt gratitude and that this meeting pledges itself not only to meet the stipulation of the committee, but, if possible, to collect an amount equal to the difference between the grant and *two thousand pounds.*" It was decided to make the effort in the early part of June. The date was extended by a resolution passed on the 29th June, at a meeting over which Rev. Henry Daniel, superintendent of the circuit, presided. At this meeting it was resolved to raise two thousand pounds, exclusive of the grant, and further to secure, if possible, upon a reasonable extension of time, subscriptions to pay off the *whole* debt. Tuesday, the 7th of July, was fixed for the contemplated effort. A thousand notices of the meeting were sent to pew-holders and others worshipping in the four chapels, and the ministers were requested to publish a notice of the meeting in the fullest manner on the ensuing Sabbath. A statement was prepared showing the chapel debt to be £3,950, principally in promissory notes, on which a large amount of interest had accumulated. From this statement it would appear that the creditors were chiefly our own Methodist preachers who had made advances to the trustees. The effort was made and the sum of £1,336 11s. 8d. was subscribed, of which, in a very short time, £1,298 18s. 1d. were paid. Messrs. G. T. Ray, Henry Whiteside and James Smith each subscribed £100, and Messrs. R. Whiteside, Mark Varley, George King, William Hamilton and Aaron Eaton gave £50 each. These were the largest amounts. The other sums subscribed ranged from the lowest amount mentioned down to, in one case, a single penny. Measured by the amount of self-denial involved, perhaps the noblest subscriptions were among the smaller amounts. There were one hundred and eighty-two subscribers, and of these the only persons now worshipping in the church are Samuel Gardner, J. J. Munroe, Jos. Pritchard, James Sullivan and R. W. Thorne.

The fund was supplemented by public collections in the churches; Centenary contributing £74 6s. 1d., and Germain street £34 16s. 10d. The question of holding a tea meeting was considered. There were two dissentient voices, but the others being in favor of it, it was held. The tickets were to be one dollar, but the price was reduced to fifty cents, and the sum of £79 8s. 1d. realized.

From the *Observer*, of December 23rd, 1845, we learn that " some unprincipled wretch broke into the Centenary Wesleyan chapel last night in this city, and took away some seven or eight pounds in money, which had been left by the stewards in one of the closets inside the communion table. They were so scrupulous as to the coin that a pile of coppers not current here were conscientiously left on the floor; and so hasty in their pillaging that a pair of silver cups presented to the Wesleyan society by the late John Ferguson, Esq., and used on sacramental occasions at this chapel, escaped their searching eye. They had visited the school-room last week and stole of the childrens' money about six dollars; having made a second search there fruitlessly and being very needy they forced their way to the upper part of the edifice, violently breaking open the doors with no tender feelings as to the damage they were doing to the mouldings."

In recent years the cupidity of some individual has manifested itself, as in the above item, though without the violence used by that thief; the occasion being the stealing of quite a sum of money representing the savings of the members of Miss Fannie Henderson's society class. These young ladies, imbued with the very worthy motive of reducing the debt on the present church, adopted a plan of systematic saving, and accumulating quite a respectable amount deposited it in what they thought was a safe place in the church. The eye of sinful man, however, discovered their treasure and it was carried away.

Upon another occasion, in late years, a man was caught by a lady class-leader in the act of carrying away one of the large Bibles from the church. It was with difficulty, and only by the assistance of outside help, that he was compelled to relinquish the book.

The large bell of the old church having fallen in the great fire was removed to the Varley school lot, and being of such great weight the trustees had no thought but that it was safe where it was. Such, however, was not the case, as it was unlawfully removed and is supposed to have been sold as old metal.

In 1846 Rev. H. Daniel and Rev. T. Sutcliffe were appointed to Saint John,—the former being superintendent. Leaders' meetings were regularly held, and from the minutes it would appear that Mr. Daniel was faithful in his exhortation to the leaders as to their duties; attendance at class was insisted upon, and at this time the cause seemed to be very prosperous. The following minutes would indicate somewhat the nature of the business done at these meeting:

TUESDAY EVENING, 21st November, 1848.
Present: Rev. Henry Daniel, Messrs. S. Bayard, D. Collins, G. Whittaker, J. Emison, Henry Marshall, James Sullivan,

Jacob Wilson, Joseph Dougan. The following persons were reported sick : Mrs. Maxwell, Mrs. Jones and Mrs. Crowthers. Copies of the annual address of the conference were distributed to the leaders and stewards, who were notified by the preacher of the direction of conference to read the rules of society once in each quarter in full class. After some excellent remarks from the preacher on the duties of the leaders, the meeting was closed with prayer by Brother Dougan.

At a meeting held on 12th October, 1846, it was decided to have the grade of the gallery seats altered at a cost not to exceed £50. It would appear that the elevation of these seats was of a pitch considered ridiculous.

On the 15th April, 1847, the following resolution was adopted : " Whereas, it appears (after a careful investigation of the financial state of the Centenary chapel and of its prospective income), that with proper management it will in the future meet its ordinary expenditure, as well as the interest accruing on the remaining debt of about £1,700, the trustees have much pleasure in yielding up the ordinary Sabbath collections to the district meeting, to be again applied to their legitimate uses, and in doing so they cannot forego the opportunity of expressing their grateful acknowledgments for the bestowment of these collections in the past, through which the chapel was probably saved from very much difficulty and embarassment." In reply the following extract, from the district minutes, was sent :

"DISTRICT ROOM, Sackville, July 26, 1847.

"*Centenary Chapel, Saint John.* A communication from the trustees of the Centenary chapel acknowledging the kindness of the district meeting in permitting the appropriations of the Sunday collections of that chapel for the last four years towards the payment of their chapel expenses ; and announcing the pleasing information that the chapel was now placed, by a special effort of our Saint John friends and a grant from the Wesleyan Missionary Committee, in circumstances in which they no longer need those collections, and that they will replace them among the resources of the circuit.

"*Resolved*, That this meeting congratulate the trustees of the Centenary chapel on the success of their endeavors to reduce their liabilities, and although the brethren have suffered much on account of having to relinquish a large amount annually, for the last four years, in the non-payment of their own acknowledged and long established allowances, they regret not the aid thus extended to the trustees as it has afforded an opportunity of proving their affection for the cause of God; and they doubt not that the influence of their example will long be felt by our friends in Saint John.

"WILLIAM TEMPLE, Secretary."

During the year 1848 gas was introduced into the church.

The last trustee meeting of Centenary board, presided over by Mr. Daniel, was held on May 7th, 1849. At this meeting Mr. LeSueur, being about to remove from the city, resigned the trustee stewardship, and Mr. E. Lloyd was appointed in his place.

At a quarterly meeting held on the 16th May a petition, signed by eighty pewholders and members of the congregation, asking that the board should request a re-appointment of Mr. Daniel to the circuit for the fourth year, was presented and complied with. For some reason Mr. Daniel was not sent back to Saint John, but in his place Rev. Richard Knight was appointed, and with him came Rev. Mr. Cooney to Centenary.

In a memoir of Dr. Knight, written by his son, it is said in reference to his Saint John appointment: "This appointment was attended with peculiar communications of comfort and hope to his own soul, and on arriving there he found the society prosperous, and many of the members 'living in possession of perfect love.' His anticipations of good were fully realized, as he was privileged in the second year of his ministry to witness a singularly gracious revival, which continued with little cessation for more than two years."

In March, 1853, he wrote to the *Provincial Wesleyan:* "The most extensive and permanent revivals ever recorded have been those which originated in the church. Much may be reasonably hoped for when more than ordinary divine influence begins at the *house of God.* Thus it was in the present gracious visitation, with which the Lord has been pleased to bless us in this city." Many of the members were taught of the spirit to experience the privilege and power of entire sanctification. Following a lucid exposition of this Christian doctrine, he remarks: "A sanctified ministry and a sanctified church should be the motto of all the lovers of Zion, and to this both ministers and people should continually aspire."

In this year (1849) there was a very serious disturbance in the Home conference, owing to the insubordination of some eight or ten ministers, who, through the medium of what were known as "Fly Sheets," made shameful attacks upon the officers of the conference, particularly Drs. Bunting and Newton. A strict and deserved application of the discipline terminated their connection, but not without scattering many thousands of members and separating them from our communion.

At a meeting of the Saint John (south) quarterly board held on 29th May, at which there were twenty-seven members present, it was moved by J. M. Hamilton and seconded by G. A. Lockhart, that the following resolution be signed by the circuit and society stewards and handed to Rev. Mr. Knight to forward to the home conference:

"From a sense of duty which we owe to the executive of our body in England, as also from a sincere regard to the interests of that form of Christianity called 'Wesleyan Methodism,' we, the trustees, local preachers, stewards and leaders, office-bearers in the Wesleyan church connected with the Germain street and Centenary Wesleyan chapels in quarterly meeting assembled, do hereby unanimously agree in expressing our approbation of the course adopted by the conference of 1849 in the expulsion of certain ministers from connection with that body, whose subsequent conduct has fully proved to all right-thinking persons the justice of the course adopted with them ; and likewise further agree in manifesting our perfect confidence in the integrity of the missionary committee, treasurer and secretaries. While with feelings of painful interest we have viewed the conduct of the expelled, so calculated to lead astray the weak minded and unwary, we cannot but rejoice in the belief that their machinations, far from injuring our beloved Zion, will rather tend to benefit her spiritually, numerically and financially.

"Signed on behalf of quarterly meeting,

"R. WHITESIDE, Circuit Steward,
"G. P. SANCTON,
"W. A. ROBERTSON,
"R. W. THORNE,
"T. C. HUMBERT,
} Society Stewards.

On the 5th October in this year Mark Varley died ; having the day before made his will, under which he directed that his share or interest in the vessel "El Dorado," and his lots of land on Dock street and in Lower Cove, should be sold and the proceeds applied to the establishment and maintenance of a day school under the supervision of the trustees of the Wesleyan Methodist church in the city of Saint John. The trustees, at the time of his death, were Gilbert T. Ray, George A. Lockhart, George Whittaker, John B. Gaynor, Edward E. Lockhart, David Collins, Richard Whiteside, senr., Henry Whiteside, Edward T. Knowles, James Smith, Richard W. Thorne, Edward Lloyd, Daniel J. McLaughlin, senr., William Till, Aaron Eaton, George P. Sancton, William A. Robertson, John Gardner, Michael Thompson, Colin E. Gross, Robert Salter, Isaac Olive, James Olive, William Beattie, G. B. Vaughan, J. J. Clarke, Zachariah Adams, Benjamin Tibbits, William O. Theal, Thomas Thompson and John Jordan. Mr. Varley had been a member of Centenary church and a pew-holder therein from its dedication until the time of his death, which occurred in his forty-seventh year. He was a native of Hull, England, and he who searches for Mr. Varley's reputation will find it truthfully inscribed on his monument in the Rural cemetery: "That during a residence in Saint John of thirty-four years spent in honorable industry, he was universally esteemed for kindness of disposition and strict integrity." From the proceeds of the sale of the property above mentioned a lot of land was purchased from the trustees of Centenary church; a substantial building erected thereon, and the Varley Wesleyan Day School established for the purpose of imparting instruction to pupils of both sexes, entirely free from all religious denominational restriction. This school was maintained by the income arising from the original bequest; from moderate tuition fees, and from grants, in some years quite liberal, from the Provincial Legislature, and continued as a most effective institution until the free school system was introduced, when the school trustees leased it for the purpose of public schools.

In the fall of 1850 the Centenary trustees, deeming it desirable for the better accommodation of the congregation as well as for the general appearance of the building, decided to alter the entrance and change the front of the building. An outline of the changes being a wooden platform supported by pillars, to be erected on the outside of the building extending the whole length from east to west, terminating in steps of the same material at each end. The whole to be enclosed by an iron balustrade and gates; the rock being previously cut away and the retaining wall faced with brick. An entrance to the basement under the platform and two windows to be provided.

In January of the following year the trustees, while deeming it essential that the proposed changes should be undertaken, yet felt it to be of primary importance that the existing debt should be reduced. Messrs. Smith, McLaughlin and Ray were appointed a committee to suggest ways and means. A gracious revival soon began and the enterprise for a season was delayed. In June, however, the work was undertaken. An appeal was made to both congregations; circulars placed in the pews of each church, and the trustees of Germain street invited to seats on the platform in Centenary at the public meeting. The meeting was held on the 19th June. The trustees from Germain street did not attend as requested, but there were on the platform Rev. Messrs. Knight and Cooney and the Centenary trustees. The following statement was read :

Amount of debt on the chapel at the time of the
  special effort in 1846......................£4,198 15s. 9d.
Amount raised by such effort, in-
  cluding tea meeting..........£1,309 6s. 11d.
Weekly collections and other
  sources.... ....   312 10   6
Received from Home Conference   600 0   0   2,221 17   5
                                              —————————
  Present debt............   £1,976 18s. 4d.

As a result of this meeting £759 12s. 6d. was contributed, and the steward says : "The result is highly gratifying. We expect to increase the amount to £1,000, and it shows the generous expansive character of our beloved Methodism, and that God, even our own God, delights as ever in his people. To Him, indeed, be the glory."

The sum of £27 9s. 5d. was afterwards contributed from a meeting held in Germain street chapel,—which was supplemented by a donation from Mrs. Bradley of £200; from Miss McGee of £25 and from a lady in Nova Scotia of £9. Just at this time a sale of one lot and release of another to the Varley school trust, added £440 to the trust funds.

Having been so successful in the reduction of the debt, the question of improvements was again considered. The plans that had been approved, and which subsequently in 1876 were practically carried out, were now abandoned, and, amid considerable opposition, it was decided to have an inside entrance instead of one from the outside. The improvements were effected at a cost of £386 14s. 6d., and from that time till 1876 the entrance was from the basement on the inside. The thanks of the board were tendered to their esteemed friend and brother, Aaron Eaton, Esq., for "his personal oversight; his efficient and gratuitous services during a period of some months in superintending the repairs, by which the comfort, convenience and solidity of the edifice were conserved, praying also that the issue of it might be blessings to him and his, especially in their more hallowed enjoyments whilst worshipping in the building."

At a meeting of stewards and leaders of the Centenary held on Monday evening, 19th April, the appointment of the following officers and visitors in connection with the Sabbath school was confirmed. Mention is made of this because it is the first record of the kind there is in the books, though the school had been organized some years before :—

John Gardner, superintendent ;
John Jenkins, assistant superintendent ;
George P. Sancton, secretary ;
J. V. Troop, teachers' librarian ;
Gilbert Bent, scholars' librarian ;
Mathew Thomas,
Robert Hannah,
George Hardy,
W. J. Starr,
S. Manaton,
Geo. P. Sancton.
} Visitors.

Mr. Cooney, having been three years in Centenary, was appointed to Milltown. He has given us, in an interesting autobiography, some reminiscences of his pastorate, and, as his book is quite rare, extracts from it will be appreciated. He says: "In Saint John South we spent three very happy years; as happy and useful as we expect to enjoy while the Lord permits us to labor in His name. I was associated in colleagueship with the Rev. Richard Knight, chairman of the district." (He had been previously, in the year 1835, associated with Mr. Knight in Halifax.) "We labored harmoniously and successfully. These three years were the most prosperous, both in spirituals and temporals, that this station, the most important in the eastern provinces, ever enjoyed. To the glory of God we record it. Both the congregations and the societies were increased; the chapel debts were liquidated and large sums expended upon painting and repairing the chapels. The first year we brought to the district a surplus of more than eighty pounds; the second year nearly one hundred pounds, and the third year, if I mistake not, about one hundred and fifty pounds.

"I never felt more sensibly, than on this important station, how great a matter it is for a Methodist preacher to have a suitable wife. Mrs. Cooney was rendered a great blessing to the church in Saint John, and much of the influence I possessed was derived, under God, from her zeal, her prudence and piety. All the time we were in this circuit, she met a very large and flourishing class, gathered up from the congregation by herself; she also taught the female Bible class in the Sabbath school, and served to the utmost of her ability in sustaining and extending the operations of the Dorcas society. Our parting from these dear people was a sore trial to us; and, take them all in all, perhaps we will never meet their like again."

Upon revisiting the city in the following year, he makes reference to the churches and people, and says: " Preached in Germain street in the forenoon and in the Centenary church in the evening. Morning congregation large, and in the evening the house was crowded. After the evening service we held a prayer meeting in the basement story at which, probably, from five to six hundred persons were present. The Lord was in their midst; His arm was made bare, and his saving power displayed."

Mr. William Wright, of the well-known firm of William and Richard Wright, lived on Brussels street,—in a house yet standing though said to be the oldest in that section of the city. He was exceedingly hospitable and kind to the Methodist ministers visiting the city, many of whom, Mr. Cooney among the number, often made their home with him. He was a member of the Centenary church and manifested much interest in it. Mr. Cooney, after making some kind reference to him and his family, says: " There are many others of whose Christian courtesy and kindness we have largely partaken, but want of space and many other circumstances renders it impossible to do more than gratefully acknowledge it. It would be almost criminal were we to omit the names of our dear friends, 'the poor steward' and his generous and hospitable wife,—we allude to Mr. and Mrs. Richard Thorne. Their house was our last resting place in New Brunswick. Their dear faces were among the last we saw, and should we never see them again on earth, we hope to meet them in heaven. To these beloved friends in Christ, and to Mr. and Mrs. Aaron Eaton, in whose dwelling we found our first New Brunswick home, we now present our lively and grateful re-remembrance."

Mr. Cooney, as is well known, had previously to joining the Methodist society, been a Roman Catholic. He was converted under Rev. Enoch Wood, to whose memory and to the memory of Messrs. McNutt and Pickles, he pays a high tribute. He is said to have been a powerful preacher, being particularly effective in his powers of description. As a lecturer he was also very popular, and frequently occupied the Mechanics' Institute platform. Older members of the community often speak of his addresses at Bible society gatherings and temperance meetings as most powerful efforts.

In a recent letter to the writer, Mrs. Cooney says: "I believe my dear husband's memory is still green among our many Saint John friends. The five years we spent between the city and Carleton were among the happiest of our itinerant life. My love for that dear people has not grown cold. It has been kept alive and warm when memory is active in presenting the many proofs of disinterested love and affection."

On the 19th May, 1852, Rev. Mr. Knight, in a meeting of the quarterly board, at which there were twenty-seven members present, put the following question: Is it expedient in the opinion of this meeting that there should be another chapel built within the limits of the Saint John South Circuit? To which there was a unanimous response of, Yes! This decided, the meeting entered upon the consideration of another subject. Mr. Cardy having been called to the chair, Mr. Ray and others addressed the meeting on the subject, if practicable, of procuring the labors of Rev. Mr. Knight for another year. It was understood that the meeting did not wish in any way to wound the feelings of any preacher, or to find fault with any one that in the wisdom of the district might be appointed to the circuit. It would seem that the district acquiesced, for Mr. Knight came for the fourth year, and with him Rev. John Allison, whose work was to be in connection with Centenary.

Mention has been made of the decision of the quarterly board as to the expediency of erecting another chapel. On the 1st September, 1852, Messrs. Geo. Whittaker and Geo. A. Lockhart were appointed to wait upon the Hon. Charles Simonds to ascertain if the lot on Vinegar Hill, adjoining lot on Brussels street owned by trustees, could be purchased.

This committee afterwards reported : "Saw Mr. Simonds ; " would sell the lot in question on time for £150 to the trustees ; " time of payment immaterial as long as interest at the rate of " six per cent. was paid. Would take, instead of mortgage, the " joint notes of any two or three of the trustees, or if preferred " to pay cash would make discount of £18, making price £132."

A committee was appointed to solicit subscriptions on basis of building a church costing from £1,000 to £1,250. The matter was further considered at a meeting held in the singing room of Centenary church on 27th May, 1853, when the following resolutions were adopted, moved by Brother S. Bayard, seconded by Brother R. Hannah :

1. That it is deemed necessary that a chapel be built on our property in Exmouth street.

2. That the building be of sufficient size to accommodate 800 persons.

3. That the cost of the same be limited to £1,500.

4. That a committee of three be appointed to obtain sub-

scriptions; to commence their operations after the first Sabbath in July, on which day public notice will be given.

With this meeting another conference year closes, and the officials seem very loth to lose the services of Mr. Knight, who had been already at Saint John for four years, and the following resolution, as a suggestion to the district meeting, was adopted. Moved by Brother Fraser, seconded by Brother Hannah:

"This quarterly meeting cannot separate without expressing their gratitude to God for the blessed effects which have attended the labors of Rev. Mr. Knight during the four years he labored on this circuit, and in view of the present aspect of Methodist interests in this city, this meeting thinks it very desirable that the chairman should be stationed in the immediate vicinity of Saint John."

The resolution was addressed to the Wesleyan Missionaries comprising the district meeting at Fredericton. The suggestion was accepted and Mr. Knight was appointed to Carleton, or Saint John West. This did not sever his intercourse with a people to whom he was attached by the strongest bonds of affection. The proximity of his new sphere enabled him to continue his pastoral visitation among them,—an employment he greatly cherished wherever his lot was cast. So abiding, too, was their confidence, as well as that of his brethren, in his administrative wisdom, that he was always consulted in important circuit affairs.

Rev. Mr. Hennigar was sent as superintendent of circuit for that year, and Rev. Mr. Cardy accompanied him to minister to Centenary, where he remained for three years. Rev. James Taylor was sent as the third preacher, in compliance with the request of the quarterly board. There seemed some doubt as to what section Mr. Taylor was to look after, and, in addition to labors in the city, he had also been assigned to work in the surrounding country. The quarterly meeting insisted that he should confine his attention to work in the city and a committee was appointed to secure a place in which to hold services, as near the site of the proposed church on Exmouth street as possible. Mr. Taylor's labors were, however, divided between the city and the country.

On the 18th July, 1853, a meeting of the two congregations had been held in Centenary, at which the views of the quarterly board were explained in reference to the new building about to be erected, and subscriptions made towards the building fund.

In the next year, 29th May, 1854, a deficiency of £29 3s. 1d. was reported, caused by the salary of the third preacher and expenses incurred in purchasing new furniture for Mission House; £24 were subscribed at the quarterly meeting and the balance, £5 3s. 1d., was paid by Mr. G. P. Sancton. On several occasions deficiencies like this were met in this way, and not made a charge on the income of the next year. At this meeting it was resolved that, owing to the expansion of the work in this city, the district meeting be requested to furnish for the Saint John South Circuit, exclusively, a third preacher,—a young man free of incumbrances is strongly urged.

In September, 1853, the first notice of an organ appears. It was then reported that the instrument was on its way from England. A large amount had been subscribed for the organ fund and a tea meeting was about to be held, proceeds of which were to be applied to that purpose. Up to this time the official consent of the trustees had not been given. There was a feeling on the part of some of the trustees adverse to its admission, and at the first meeting called to consider the matter there was much discussion. The further consideration was to be had at "an early adjourned meeting, at which all the trustees might be present, to calmly consider what, if not kindly and considerately dealt with, might prove of serious injury to our hitherto harmonious people."

At the next meeting, after a protracted discussion, the sense of the meeting was taken, when there appeared for its admission three, and against, three. The trustees being equally divided, the Rev, J. G. Hennigar, superintendent of the circuit, gave his casting vote in its favor, at the same time expressing his reasons and regret at being compelled to do so. It was agreed to admit the organ on the understanding that it should entail no expense on the trust. The steward was opposed to its admission. It is supposed that the question was dealt with kindly and considerately, as there is no record of the harmony having been disturbed.

Those who were opposed to the organ managed, for five years, to hold the others to the understanding upon which it was admitted into the church; whilst the committee, to whom it was entrusted, sought to be relieved of responsibility. The trustees would not make provision for the organist's salary, neither would they pay for insurance on the instrument. In 1856 the organ debt was £190. The trustees, beginning to show magnaminity, undertook to pay the interest on that sum if the committee would see that the debt was removed in eighteen months. They also agreed to pay half the expenses entailed for fires, etc., on evenings when the choir assembled for practice. With these concessions the recalcitrants began to lose ground, and in 1859 it was ordered that the balance due the organ committee should be paid out of the proceeds of the sale of some pews which had been added to the church. The vote was four to three. This conclusion was not reached without one of the brethren requesting that his solemn protest might be recorded against such action, as it was not only contrary to the oft-repeated decision of the board, but in his humble opinion adverse to the spiritual worship of God, especially in the singing part [of the service. The chapel steward then rose and reminded the trustees of his anxiety to see the debt reduced, which the action of the evening had placed more distant than ever, and also of his former expressed determination that should such a decision be arrived at, he would feel it his duty to resign his stewardship, which he accordingly did. Mr. Lloyd was present, however, at the next meeting as steward, and served faithfully for years after and until his removal from the city took place.

To practice on the organ was regarded as quite a favor, and none were allowed the privilege without special permission. Moreover, quite a sharp eye was kept on the choir to see that they did not offend. Upon one occasion the minister in charge drew the attention of the trustees to the fact that the choir were in the habit of practising after service on Sunday. The trustees agreeing with the minister that the act was very reprehensible, it was resolved to instruct the leader to discontinue the same.

In April, 1854, the declaration was made that the following persons were the trustees of the church :

R. Whiteside,		D. J. McLaughlin,	
E. T. Knowles,	Original.	James Smith,	New.
G. T. Ray,		R W. Thorne,	
D. Collins,		E. Lloyd,	

At the next meeting Mr. Fraser appeared before the trustees, on behalf of city temperance organizations, requesting the use of the church for one evening during a great demonstration to be held in the city in the following month. He promised that great care would be taken of the property in pews ; that the people should be admitted by ticket, and objectionable characters kept out ; but would not undertake to say that applause or other demonstration of feeling would not be indulged in.

Whereupon the trustees, having expressed their opinion as to the propriety of allowing a building set apart for the worship of God to be opened to meetings of a secular character, took time to consider and at the next meeting, by a vote of five to three, withheld permission.

The trustees recognizing that the church had been dedicated for the worship of God, for years held to their declaration with an exactness that was truly conservative. Many applications were made for the use of the church, but no matter how much the trustees were in sympathy with the object, they adhered strictly to their resolution to allow nothing but what was of a religious service to take place within its walls. This supports an observation made in an early part of this paper, that in those days a tea meeting was regarded as a means of grace, for be it remembered that the tea meeting was a time-honored institution among the people of this congregation.

In 1861 Mr. McMurray applied for the use of the church for a lecture by Mr. Narraway, in aid of a brother minister who had been burned out at Sussex. The request was not granted and the lecture was given in Mr. Smith's hall on Prince William street.

In 1862 the Reform Society made application for the use of the basement for a temperance meeting in connection with a great gathering that was to be held in the city. The trustees, or a majority of them at least, though deeply in sympathy with the temperance movement, did not think it consistent with the purposes for which the church was dedicated and would not allow the use of the basement for that purpose.

In 1864 Mr. Narraway applied, on behalf of the Home Missionary Society, for the use of the church in which to deliver a lecture in aid of the funds of the society, but the loyalty of the trustees to their original resolution was such that permission was not granted.

In 1865 application was again made for use of the basement in which a temperance lecture might be given, and the record is "all appeared to be of one sentiment favorable to the cause, but reluctant to grant the use of the place asked, it being their opinion that a church was not the proper place for such purpose. However, to avoid offence and in deference to the feelings of others, the trustees waived their own and, trusting it would be the last application, and in no way consenting that it should be regarded as a precedent, granted permission." This may be regarded as the entering wedge.

On 11th July, 1867, a meeting was called to consider the advisability of allowing the use of the church for two lectures to be delivered by Dr. Lachlan Taylor and Dr. Stevenson, who were delegates to the conference from the Canada conference. Much discussion took place,—reference being made to former decisions which were very peremptory against the use of the place of worship for any such purpose; but permission was granted, the steward only voting against it.

On July 6th, 1868, Rev. William Morley Punshoon delivered his celebrated lecture, "John Wesley and his Times." Upon this occasion there was no dissent to the use of the church, and from that time the resolution, to which for so long a time there was so much loyalty, was not strictly applied, and in later years very considerable latitude has been shown.

At a trustee meeting held in April, 1854, the steward reported that there were £100 in the Commercial Bank to the credit of the trustees, which was considered a gratifying turn in the financial position of the chapel.

To return to the meetings of the quarterly board we find that although the district meeting promised to send a young man, who might be free from incumbrances, to assist the ministers in the city, yet they allowed the year to go by without making the appointment,—perhaps just such an one as was asked for was not available. In the next year further action was taken, and on 29th May, 1855, the following resolution was adopted: "The quarterly meeting having their attention called to the great loss in consequence of the duties of the circuit being altogether too onerous for two ministers; therefore *Resolved*, That we again direct the attention of the district meeting to the promise made by them to us last year in the appointment of a third preacher to the city." In response to this Rev. Charles Stewart was sent.

The year 1855 was one of importance to the Wesleyans in these provinces, and the church passed through a great and important change. Hitherto they had been nursed and cherished by the Missionary committee. Now the districts resolved to relieve the committee of the burthen, and in July of this year, at Halifax, the measure was carried into effect through the agency of Rev. Dr. Beecham, whom the conference sent out for that purpose. The conference of Eastern British America was thus formed. At this time in the bounds of the conference there were—71 central or principal stations, called circuits, with 208 chapels; 88 ministers; 109 local preachers; 12,540 full and accredited members; 139 Sabbath schools, and 8,192 scholars.

In the following year conference was held in the Centenary. Dr. Beecham was expected to be present and preside, but shortly before the assembling his death occurred. The conference proceeded with its duties amid the gloom cast upon it by the sad loss they had sustained. Out of respect to the memory of one who was much beloved and so prominent in the connexion, the pulpit of the church was draped in black for a season.

Rev. Mr. Stewart's labors were so appreciated in Saint John that in the next year he was invited as the second minister. The invitation included Revs. C. Churchill, C. Stewart and D. D. Currie. The conference, however, appointed Rev. Messrs.

Botterell, Albrighton and Stewart. As a preacher Mr. Albrighton held a high rank, being both eloquent and attractive. His ministrations in every way were entirely satisfactory; during his term the congregations were very large, and the cause was greatly strengthened.

From the month of October, 1855, until the opening of Exmouth street church, in January, 1857, service was held in Benevolent Hall. This building was erected by the late D. J. McLaughlin and still exists. Owing to changed circumstances, and the necessities not being what they were, it is not now used for the purpose for which it was built. It has been very useful in its day, and in it for years services were regularly held; a most successful Sabbath school conducted, and much good effected.

In the year 1856 Henry Marshall, G. Bent, G. P. Sancton and W. H. Harrison were elected trustees of Centenary church. In this year the big bell broke whilst being rung and measures were taken to replace it.

On the 20th May, 1857, at a quarterly meeting, the disposition of stewards and leaders was finally arranged, and was as follows:

Germain Street—T. C. Humbert, R. Hannah, F. Harrison, Geo. Whittaker, G. T. Ray, Thomas Furness, Robert Elsdon, Jacob Wilson, David Collins, William Till, James Emison, William Brent.

Centenary—Geo. P. Sancton, R. W. Thorne, R. Whiteside, Edward Lloyd, Henry Marshall, Jno. Gardner, Jas. Sullivan, E. E. Lockhart, Jno. Jenkins, E. T. Knowles, Jno. Bradley, J. P. Taylor, T. M. Albrighton (the minister's class), A. Eaton, R. G. Hall, Hugh Rennick.

Exmouth Street—Wm. Clawson, J. T. Smith, Jas. Lemon, R. Riggs, D. Sullivan, H. Graham, Jno. Ennis, H. Cochran.

Rev. Mr. Botterell reported 707 persons meeting in class in the Saint John South Circuit.

On the 18th November in this year, a prayer meeting was established for official members only and was regularly held for some time on Wednesday evenings.

The conference of next year, 1858, appointed Rev. Messrs. Botterell, William Wilson and Albrighton to Saint John. In the fall of that year two gentlemen, who had long been connected with the society, were removed from it by death,—we refer to Gilbert T. Ray and Richard Whiteside. Their active interest in and prominent connection with the society call for something more than a passing notice. Mr. Ray died on October 23rd, after having been for many years identified with the Methodist church. He was deeply interested in all Missionary enterprises. He was one of the original trustees of Centenary church; a class-leader and superintendent of the Sabbath school in connection with Germain street, and for some years circuit steward of the Saint John South Circuit. His interest in the city churches and connexional funds was manifested both by generous gifts, and a deep concern in all matters which to any extent affected them. He was conservative in his views and did not quickly leave the old paths. His caution was of great service in his time, and many people were influenced very much by the opinions of Gilbert T. Ray. In a fortnight after the death of Mr. Ray, Mr. Whiteside quietly and peacefully entered into rest. He joined the church in 1832, and two years later succeeded Mr. Ray as circuit steward, which office he continued to hold until the time of his death; though during late years, by reason of his infirmities, the duties were largely performed by Geo. P. Sancton. Mr. Whiteside's records are a marvel of neatness. The circuit book so long committed to his trust, with its faultless penmanship and stainless pages, remains as a memory of his order, diligence and carefulness, and constitute a pattern worthy the imitation of his successors in office. As a class-leader for nearly twenty years he was most zealous and exemplary. He was invariably in his place a quarter-of-an-hour before the time appointed for meeting that he might, by prayerful meditation, prepare himself for the exercises which lay before him. Mr. Sancton succeeded Mr. Whiteside, and most efficiently discharged his official duties for upwards of ten years, or so long as he remained connected with Centenary. Mr. Sancton gave much time and attention to the duties of his office; always manifested a great interest in the affairs of the church. His genialty made him very popular with his brethren and the members of the congregation; acting as an usher he felt it to be a privilege to extend kindly greetings to the stranger as he came within our gates, and in no church would a visitor receive more hospitable attention or kindlier greetings from its ushers than would be extended to him by George P. Sancton.

In 1859 it was decided to remove the north gallery and finish those on the sides to the end; the vestry below on the one side and the back stair entrance on the other side to be removed; the pulpit to be moved back to the wall and constructed on a new design, and the square pews around the altar to be changed into single pews. These changes were made at a cost of £126 8s. 5d. The additional pews given, by reason of the alterations, being sold brought £341. It was out of this balance that the debt on the organ was paid.

On the evening of February 2nd, 1859, a united meeting in the interest of the Methodist Sabbath schools was held in the Germain street church. At this meeting the claim was made that while Robert Raikes was the founder of Sabbath schools, yet he could not primarily be considered the originator of the scheme; the latter honor belonged to an old Methodist woman who had long lived on what was called "The Green," in the city of Gloucester, England, where the children were in the habit of assembling every Lord's day. Moved with compassion for them, earnestly did she pray that God might be pleased to employ her in some way to be useful to them. She succeeded in getting them in her house and interested them in Scripture stories, illustrating her talk with pictures she had. In this way she soon found that God was answering her prayer. Mr. Raikes was editor of the Gloucester *Journal*, and hearing of the incident went to visit the old lady, with the result that the light from heaven lit up his spirit. Three facts were claimed at this meeting: First, that above mentioned; second, to a Methodist then living was Saint John indebted for its first Sunday school; third, to a few Methodists and Baptists of Saint John was the temperance world indebted for its first total abstinence society.

On Tuesday, 27th December, 1859, the jubilee of Germain street chapel was observed. The church was appropriately trimmed. There were banners in various places bearing the names of persons who had been prominent in church work in the city. Rev. Messrs. Wilson, Botterell, England and Lathern were present, and took part in the exercises. The meeting was also addressed by one of the fifteen who helped prepare the foundation. Sixty voices in the choir were led by John Humbert. The singing was in accordance with old times, and the tunes were those in "Humbert's Notes,"—a book published by Stephen Humbert, father of the then leader, who also led the choir from the first for many years.

The appointments for the next year, 1860, were: Revs. J. McMurray, Wm. Wilson and John Lathern as first, second and third ministers. The society, and Centenary church in particular, sustained a loss in this year by the removal of Henry Marshall to Fredericton. He had been assistant to the trustee-steward for many years and was, indeed, a very great help to that officer. Besides being a trustee of Centenary, he had been for a long time a member of the quarterly board of the circuit. In view of his removal, and as a "slight token of esteem and regard entertained for him as a Christian and a brother," the quarterly board presented him with a Bible and hymn book, in which a suitable inscription was placed by the superintendent and circuit steward.

The society also met with another loss by the death of John Bradley, a member of Centenary congregation. In the minutes of the quarterly book a record is made deploring the loss and giving expression to the regard in which he was held as a Christian.

Changes in the "discipline" of the church were from time to time made by the conference, and were usually based upon memorials from quarterly boards. It would appear that the public recognition and reception given to persons joining the church possibly was the outcome of action taken at the quarterly board of Saint John South. At a meeting held in November, 1860, on motion of James Sullivan, seconded by John Fraser, it was resolved, "That conference be memorialized requesting that a public recognition be given to members coming into our church." It may be of interest to observe in this connection that in the year 1870, on motion of E. E. Lockhart, seconded by James Sullivan, at a meeting of Centenary quarterly board it was resolved, "That a memorial be presented to the next conference asking that the superintendents of Sabbath schools be made members of the quarterly boards." Each of these provisions is now found in the discipline of the Methodist church.

A new steel bell was placed in position in the tower of Centenary in 1860, and further improvements, including the painting of the entire church, were made.

In the year 1861-62 Mr. McMurray remained as superintendent; Dr. Richey and Mr. Lathern being the second and third minister, and in the next year Dr. Richey became superintendent, while Messrs. Narraway and Nicholson were the other appointments. The circuit had been desirous for some time of securing the services of Mr. Narraway and had extended to him an invitation for the year before that in which he was appointed, and although the invitation had been accepted by him yet the conference did not make the appointment. The wisdom of his appointment, in consequence of the second invitation, was manifested in the acceptance with which his pulpit and pastoral ministrations were received and the success attending his efforts. In the winter of 1862-3 a revival of considerable importance occurred, but so exacting were its demands upon Mr. Narraway's strength that his health became so impaired as to compel a rest for a season. Hoping that a sea voyage and the air of his native land would prove beneficial he left for England in the spring of 1863, accompanied by Mrs. Narraway. Returning in a short time, he again entered upon his duties, which, until the end of his term, he discharged to the satisfaction of the circuit.

On 2d of January, 1863, the death of John Ennis occurred. Mr. Ennis was "a man of many virtues," a useful member of the community in which he lived, upright in all his dealings, and valuable in church relations. At the age of thirty-eight, as his life was opening into influence, he was called from the church militant to the church triumphant.

In the following year John Fraser, who had been contemporary with Mr. Ennis, removed from the city. In his removal the Centenary church and Methodist interests in the city generally suffered loss. He was a class leader and local preacher. In the latter capacity, just before his removal, he visited the localities in which with acceptance he had ministered to the people and left farewell messages. Having taken up his residence in Nova Scotia, he resumed the work he had relinquished in St. John. On the 13th of June, 1864, by the capsizing of a boat in the Annapolis River, near Clementsport, he was drowned. At the time of the accident Mr. Fraser was in his 46th year. He had already become a useful member of the community in which he had taken up his abode, and the cause of religion and the interests of Methodism suffered much by his sudden and sad removal.

The appointments of 1862 were not disturbed until 1864, when Mr. Addy was sent as superintendent and Mr. Brewster appointed as the third minister; Mr. Narraway remaining as the second minister. At the expiration of the year Mr. Brewster went to England. Previous to starting, the quarterly board took occasion to place on record their high appreciation of that gentleman and of his services, earnestly praying that his future course might be prosperous and useful in the cause of his divine Master. In the next year, 1865, Mr. Sponagle was sent to Saint John in the place of Mr. Brewster, while Mr. Addy remained as superintendent and Mr. Narraway was appointed for his fourth year, conference having been requested to make the appointments.

Previous to his removal the following resolution was adopted: "That the quarterly meeting respectively tender to Rev. J. R. Narraway, A. M., an expression of their high esteem for his courteous and Christian conduct in all his intercourse during the four years he has officiated on this circuit, and also their high appreciation of his eminently valuable pulpit services and pastoral care over the church generally."

In the fall of 1865 the destruction of Centenary was threatened by a fire in the immediate vicinity. As it was, considerable damage was occasioned to the northeast corner and to the end window. The insurance being promptly adjusted, the congregation suffered no loss.

Rev. James England succeeded Mr. Narraway in 1866. He was a good preacher, sound in doctrine, but in style quite different from his predecessors. He had the cause of God at heart, and his reports to the district meeting show how earnestly he sought its advancement. In his opinions he was very conservative and decided, so much so that by some he was thought to be unduly attached to them. In his administration he was brought into conflict upon a few occasions with some of his people. Probably the difficulties, which at most seem to have been trifling, were the result of the parties not understanding each other. No one who knew James England intimately could fail to recognize the purity of his mind and purposes, although perhaps at times his peculiar traits may have invested his acts with an appearance that misrepresented his meaning and motive.

On the 30th August, 1866, the death of Aaron Eaton, in the 77th year of his age, took place. From the opening of the church Mr. Eaton had been a pew-holder, though he did not become a resident of Saint John until a few months after that date. During his residence in the city he was a most active member of the Methodist church. As already stated, he declined to accept the responsibility of trusteeship, but was often consulted, and gave much time and attention to the temporal affairs of the church. On the quarterly board, a position in which he served until the time of his death, he was a valuable member. He was also deeply interested in the Exmouth street church; contributed largely of his means towards its advancement, and in every way was identified with its progress. Previous to moving to Saint John Mr. Eaton had been very active in church work in the Annapolis valley, having belonged for some years to the church at Bridgetown, which he served in almost every official relation. One does not often find reference made in the district minutes to an individual, but, under date May 31st, 1867, mention is made of Mr. Eaton as follows: "The death of Aaron Eaton, a man universally and deservedly respected for his truly Christian deportment, his deep and genuine piety, and his active and efficient discharge of the various offices he sustained, both in the circuit and connexion, leaves a blank which will not soon be filled up."

The death of Cynthia Cross took place on the 29th January, 1867. Mrs. Cross was eighty-four years of age at the time of her death, and may be said to have been contemporary with Methodism in Saint John, for the reason that when she was a little eight-year old girl the saintly Abraham Bishop, in her father's house, organized the first Methodist class and appointed her mother, Cynthia Kelley, to be the leader in the absence of the minister. We do not know at what age the daughter became a member of the church. She may have been one of those to whom Mr. Bishop had reference when he said : "The experience of the young converts is truly wonderful. Children of ten, twelve and fifteen years of age rejoice in a pardoning God." We do know that her Christian life was most exemplary. She married William Cross, whom she survived twenty-one years. She had a large family, most of whom died when young. One of her children was called Cynthia; another, Colin, — the latter was the first secretary of the Centenary Sabbath school. The husband and wife, as well as all the children, now rest in the old Methodist burial ground.

Cynthia Kelley, of whom mention has been made, died in 1829, and was buried, no doubt, in the old burial ground of this city. It would be interesting to know the exact spot, but it is as uncertain as the grave of Moses. Let us hope it is where the little children play or where the flowers grow, rather than under the ceaseless tramp of the multitude.

For years it had been felt that the perpetual change in pulpit work, as carried out by the joint pastorate, was not good. The ministers were never at rest. The plan was considered by them as unfavorable to pastoral efficiency and the growth of ministerial influence. The connexional feeling that was conserved by reason of the joint pastorate and joint administration of the affairs of the churches did not compensate for the manifest advantages incident to independent relations. At the quarterly meeting held in March, 1867, pursuant to notice given at the previous meeting, the advisability of erecting three separate and distinct circuits was considered, and after much discussion, on a vote of thirteen to six, it was resolved, "That in the opinion of this meeting it is desirable, for the benefit of the cause generally, that a division of the circuit be had into three distinct circuits." The infant church did not feel like accepting the responsibility that independence involved, and in that way the negative vote is explained. The subsequent understanding and arrangement, as adopted at the meeting, relieved the representatives of that church of the anxiety they may have had.

The understanding was "that whatever surplus may accrue from the quarterly meetings of the Germain street and Centenary churches will be paid over to the Exmouth street church towards the maintenance of the minister; and further that the minister of the Exmouth street church will be privileged to apply to all the churches for any deficiency from time to time that may arise."

The quarterly board being satisfied that the district meeting in its recommendation and the conference in its action would give effect to its resolution, proceeded to extend invitations for the circuits thus practically established. The invitations were to Revs. Charles Stewart and W. H. Heartz for Germain street and Exmouth street respectively. It was expected that Rev. Mr. England would retain charge of Centenary. The divisions of circuits and appointments as requested were made at the following conference. At a meeting held immediately after conference, in July, 1867, the distribution and divisions of classes, caused by the new arrangement, was apportioned as follows (the cause at Mispeck having been assigned to Centenary and Golden Grove to Germain street):

CENTENARY.		GERMAIN STREET.		EXMOUTH STREET.	
	No.		No.		No.
John Jenkins	10	D. Collins	30	W. W. Warwick	17
Edward Lloyd (2)	11	J. Wilson	6	J. McMoran	18
Jas. Smith	7	J. Emison	9	D. Sullivan	14
Jas. Sullivan	20	Robt. Elsdon	15	Geo. Tenant	10
E. E. Lockhart	11	A. C. Wells	16	A. Anderson	18
Jos. Prichard (2)	25	John Benson	15	D. Collins	32
E. T. Knowles	8	John McMoran	14	J. Jenkinson	14
G. P. Sancton	7	The Minister	12	H. Graham	14
J. S. Turner	7	J. Prichard	8		
The Minister	15	G. G. Clarke	9		
John Gardner	8	Mrs. Hutchings	8		
F. Harrison	7	Mrs. Hennigar	17		
Mrs. Chamberlain	4	Mrs. Benson	15		
Mrs. Whiteside	29		175		
Mrs. McAllum	16	Golden Grove	5	Exmouth Street	137
	185			Centenary	214
Mispeck	29			Germain Street	180
	214		180	Total members	531

Although these divisions were made, yet the connexional feeling existed, for we find that at the meeting when the above apportionment was made, it was agreed "that there should be a united love-feast held in each church every month, say three in each quarter, to commence with Exmouth street."

Centenary is now independent, Rev. James England being the first minister appointed after the division. The quarterly board was made up, of course, as provided by the discipline. Geo. P. Sancton was appointed Circuit Stewart and Alex. Lockhart assistant.

An invitation having been extended to Rev. John Lathern he was appointed in 1868 to Centenary. Early in his term, and largely through the instrumentality of himself and Dr. Stewart, the Carmarthen street Mission was established. From the records it would appear that Centenary became responsible for three-fifths of any deficiency, to the extent of $300, that there might be incident to that undertaking.

Mr. Lathern's pastorate was very successful; he was much esteemed, his congregations were large, and the membership was continually increased during his term of service. At the expiration of the second year the following resolution was adopted : "That the members of the Centenary quarterly meeting feel that it would be becoming especially to recognize the goodness of God to them as a church for the mercies of the past Methodistic year; the entire harmony which has prevailed; the interest that has pervaded the public and social means of grace; the extension of the cause of God by the establishment of the Lower Cove Mission in which we have shared; the promptness to aid in the financial affairs of the circuit, — all call for our thankfulness to Almighty God.

"And whereas our esteemed pastor, the Rev. John Lathern, who has been our minister for the past two years, has been, by his untiring zeal and energy in the Master's work, chiefly instrumental in bringing about the present state of the circuit;

"Therefore Resolved, That this quarterly meeting request the conference to re-appoint Rev. John Lathern to the circuit for another year."

And in the next year, at the expiration of his ministerial term, it was resolved, "That the quarterly meeting tender to Rev. John Lathern their estimate of the high value in which they regard his pastoral care and ministerial services for the past three years, and extend to him our united thanks for his zealous, faithful and tender concern for the spiritual welfare of this church and people, with sincere wish that wherever his future stations may be, that he may enjoy comfort, happiness and success in the work and labor of his divine Master."

At a public meeting of the congregation held in January, 1868, the following financial statement was presented:

Debt on chapel in 1851, at time of special effort..........		£1,985
Necessary repairs, etc., since that date.................		388
		£2,373
Raised by special effort......................	£753	
Donation by Mrs. Bradley.....................	200	
Sale of lots to Varley trust....................	450	
	£1,403	
Paid off.....................................		1,373
		£1,000
Subsequently reduced by Bradley bequest.........	£300	
Small savings in church income during 16 years	300	
		600
Present debt......................................		£ 400

The finances of the church may be said then to have been in a very satisfactory state. The expenditure by the trustees was $973 annually, while their income from pew rents should have been $1,072. Nor were the affairs of the quarterly board less satisfactory.

James Smith, after having served fourteen years as a trustee, removed in 1868 to Woodstock, at which place, in a few years afterwards, he died. Mr. Sancton, of whom mention has already been made, also removed in the same year. On the nomination of Mr. Lathern the vacancies thus created were filled by the appointment of J. V. Troop and Geo. Thomas. At the same time Alex. Lockhart was appointed as an additional trustee.

The presence of Rev. William Morley Punshon, who was stationed in Toronto, had long been hoped for by the people of Saint John, and it was with great satisfaction that such a treat was extended to nearly two thousand people on Sunday, 22nd June, 1868. It is needless to say that the people were delighted with the sermon, based upon Matthew v., 16: "Let your light so shine before men, that they may see your good works, and glorify your Father which is in heaven."

On Monday evening, in the Mechanics' Institute, Mr. Punshon delivered his celebrated lecture,— subject, "Daniel in Babylon." He then proceeded to Fredericton, and, after presiding at the conference, returned to Saint John, where, on the 3rd July, in the Centenary church, he delivered his lecture on "John Wesley and his Times." The net proceeds of this lecture amounted to $347.15, and were divided equally between Centenary and Exmouth street churches.

Mr. Punshon seems to have been impressed with the singing in Centenary, as, in notes contributed by him to the London *Recorder*, he makes the statement that "the choir of Centenary church contains some of the finest voices I have heard on this continent." The choir at that time was composed of Mrs. Tuck (leader), Mrs. Brown, Miss Troop, Miss Turner, Miss McKillop and the Misses Taylor, and W. A. Lockhart, H. D. Troop, A. G. Gray, Geo. H. Smith, Asa Blakslee and Chas. Pierce.

On July 6th, 1869, Mr. E. Lloyd, who had served faithfully as chapel-steward since 7th May, 1849, resigned office, necessitated thereto by his removal to Halifax. On the eve of his departure, in recognition of his labors, he was presented by some ladies of the congregation with a case containing a gold chain and seal attached. The trustees, also, placed on record suitable resolutions in appreciation of his services and expressive of the loss sustained by his removal. Alexander Lockhart became chapel-steward, and Captain Joseph Prichard was appointed a trustee, filling the vacancy caused by Mr. Lloyd's resignation. Mr. Lockhart had previously, in the fall of 1868, been appointed circuit-steward, which position he held until December, 1875, having as his assistant J. Clawson during his term of office.

At the conference of 1871 held in Centenary among the distinguished representatives present was Jesse T. Peck, D. D., president of the Syracuse University. Dr. Peck preached on the morning of Conference Sunday, June 25th, to an immense audience. His subject was "The Blood," and his text: "And if we walk in the light, as He is in the light, we have fellowship one with another, and the blood of Jesus Christ His Son cleanseth us from all sin." The sermon was one well remembered to this day, and it is extremely doubtful if within the walls of the old sanctuary a more powerful discourse was ever delivered than that to which the people upon that occasion listened.

In 1871, upon the invitation of the quarterly board, Rev. Duncan D. Currie was appointed to the circuit. During his pastorate the congregations were large; the interest was well maintained, and much faithful work performed. A very gracious revival of religion took place, and many who joined the church then have been active members ever since. After having labored two years Mr. Currie accepted a unanimous invitation for the third year. At the conference, however, certain exigencies arose involving special work for which, it was thought, he was peculiarly fitted, and the appointment asked for by Centenary quarterly board was not made; nor was Mr. Currie set apart for the special work, but was assigned to the Charlottetown circuit.

On the 20th November, 1871, another break was made in the board of trustees by the death of Daniel J. McLaughlin, who had served since April, 1854. Mr. McLaughlin seems to have been very regular in his attendance and took an active part at the meetings, and was, indeed, a very valuable member of the board. He was spoken of in the secular press as being "an upright Christian gentleman ; just in his dealings, and benevolent of heart." He will be especially remembered as having built and maintained at considerable expense the Benevolent Hall on Waterloo street, to which reference has already been made. Nor were his contributions by any means limited to the purposes of this building, but he gave of his means liberally to the support of the church with which he was connected, and to such other objects as merited assistance.

In September, 1872, D. J. McLaughlin, junr., was appointed to the board of trustees, filling the vacancy occasioned by the death of his father.

On the 2nd December, 1872, the death of Geo. A. Lockhart occurred. Mr. Lockhart was greatly esteemed by all who enjoyed his acquaintance. He was a gentleman of genial nature and agreeable manner; a merchant of integrity and ability. For many years he had been a prominent member of the Methodist church; was a pew-holder in Centenary from the opening, and at the time of his death he had been a member of the quarterly board for many years, either of Saint John South or the Germain street circuits, — holding his position at the latter board by reason of being superintendent of the Sabbath school of that church. Mr. Lockhart had also, for a long time, been actively identified with the temperance cause; he had also, for upwards of thirty years, been a Justice of the Peace and member of the Board of Sessions, and had filled various civic offices of trust and responsibility. His death was not unlooked for, as he had been in feeble health for some time and had reached the advanced age of seventy-five years.

In 1873 Rev. Henry Pope was appointed to Centenary, succeeding Mr. Currie, and until he was laid aside by a painful illness a few months before the close of his term, enjoyed a successful pastorate. While not losing sight of spiritual growth and advancement, especially was his administration characterised by a great improvement in the financial condition of the affairs of the church.

The suggestion of the conference of the previous year,—as to the envelope system of raising money for church purposes,—was adopted, and from the first was successful. The board in previous years had been greatly hampered by the unpleasant annual occurrence of a deficiency, involving special appeals and subscriptions. The envelope system changed this experience, and in place of a deficiency there was, after paying actual liabilities belonging to what was known as classes A and B, a surplus.

The expenditure was divided into three classes, A, B and C. Class A was payable in full, and included the minister's salary and a certain amount for missionary and connexional funds. Class B was payable in full, if sufficient, after payment of class A, otherwise to share the balance *pro rata*. In this class would be included the allowance for Sabbath school purposes and additional grants to connexional and local funds. Class C was also to be paid in full, if sufficient, after paying classes A and B, otherwise to share balance *pro rata*. In this was placed a certain sum for debt extinction, new furniture and repairs; any balance still remaining was to be expended in city missions and city church extension.

A scheme for the union of the Canada Conference with that of Eastern British America having been formulated, it was ordered to be submitted to the respective quarterly boards. At a meeting of the Centenary quarterly board, held on March 12th, 1874, the chairman read the scheme and put to the meeting these questions:

1st. Is the union desirable?
2nd. Is lay delegation acceptable?
Both of these questions were answered in the affirmative.

An appreciation of Mr. Pope's services at the close of the first year was marked by a substantial donation in addition to his salary, and in the second year an increase to the stipend of $200, making the salary $1,400.

On the 16th December, 1875, Joshua Clawson, after having been assistant for a number of years, became recording steward, and has held that office until the present time.

In January, 1876, Rev. A. B. Earle, an eminent evangelist, visited Saint John and held services in different churches of several denominations, and also in the halls of the Y. M. C. A. and Mechanics' Institute. The services were of great interest and profit, and demanded so large an accommodation that finally they were chiefly held in Centenary, it having the largest seating capacity. On many occasions the building, both basement and auditorium, was densely packed with eager listeners.

Not long after this series of services the health of Mr. Pope became impaired, and resulted in serious prostration and painful illness. During his illness the sympathy of the congregation, expressed through the officials, was extended to the pastor, while his duties were discharged by Rev. Messrs. H. R. Baker, George Steel and William Tippet respectively.

In the Autumn of 1875 and early winter following very extensive repairs to the church were made at a cost of $6,789. The principal alterations were the rebuilding and embellishing of the tower and southern façade, and the provision of convenient access to the church by means of a spacious flight of steps on either side, landing in a porch to be closed by movable folding doors, which would be removed in the summer months. The entrance to the basement was not disturbed, but was under the porch leading directly from the street. It will be remembered, as previously stated, that the approach from Princess street was formerly through the basement; thence up a narrow staircase, altogether inadequate to the requirements of so large a church, extremely dangerous in the event of a fire, and generally most inconvenient to the worshippers. By the alterations the approach to the church was made by means of the outside steps communicating directly from the street to the porch on the principal floor level of the building; thence staircases, five feet wide arranged on either side, to the galleries. It had been contemplated to bring out the tower to the frontage line and build a steeple in all 175 feet high, and also to entirely renew the front; but it was considered that this would involve too great an outlay. The tower was, therefore, built around the old one, leaving the old frame-work intact. The height of the new tower, from the ground line to the summit of the pinnacle finial, was 125 feet; the principal pinnacle stood 22 feet above the highest point of the tower battlement.

The detail of the outside finish was simple and effective, and the treatment was such as to give strength and solidity of appearance to the whole building.

It was part of the scheme to carry the chancel out in the rear; to alter and renew the windows on the east and west sides, and to raise and arch the ceiling. This part of the restoration, however, was not effected. The church was painted and its appearance was, indeed, most attractive and imposing.

At the close of Mr. Pope's pastorate his health compelled him to seek supernumerary relations, and in that capacity he is now connected with Centenary church, and is known as Dr. Pope, having well-merited the degree of Doctor of Divinity conferred upon him by the Mount Allison Institutions.

Rev. Howard Sprague, having accepted an invitation extended to him by the quarterly board, succeeded Rev. H. Pope in appointment and began his pastorate on Sunday, July 16th, 1876, preaching from Collossians, i., 28: "Whom we preach, warning every man and teaching every man in all wisdom; that we may present every man perfect in Christ Jesus."

Mr. Sprague had been already stationed in Portland, and also in Germain street; he was, therefore, well-known to the people of his new charge. As a preacher he had already taken a high position, and the reputation with which he entered upon his duties was well sustained throughout his pastorate. On Sunday evening, June 17th, 1877, Mr. Sprague concluded a series of sermons on the Ten Commandments, preaching that evening on "thou shall not covet."

The announcement was made that on the next Sabbath service in that church in the evening would begin at seven o'clock instead of six.

On the next Sabbath, instead of meeting according to announcement, the people said: "Our holy and our beautiful house, where our fathers praised Thee, is burnt up with fire; and all our pleasant things are laid waste."

At noon on Wednesday, the 20th June, there were four Methodist churches and three parsonages in the city of Saint John; at midnight there was but one church and one parsonage. In its insatiable demands the fire had shown no respect for buildings, but palace and hovel, church and the place of vice alike, became tributary to its excessive greed. Of the 145 families of Centenary, 120 were burned out, and in most cases lost not only homes but places of business. Not more than fifteen families of the Germain street church saved anything of value, while the Carmarthen street Mission, with all its interests and adherents, was in the heart of the fire. As one passed through the hundreds of acres of burnt city he knew not at times in what street he was. Wending his way to where the stately and commodious Centenary had stood, and looking to the south or east or west, he saw little save cellar walls and crumbling chimneys. Near him, at the street side, the old bell,—which had assembled people for the hour of worship and joyously pealed for marriages, or dolefully tolled for funerals, or warned people to a sense of danger at a time of fire,—lay cracked and blackened, eloquent in suggestion. It had sounded its own knell. The people who had so often responded to its call, had now no retreat from the cares and toils of life in which they could offer worship. The officials of Exmouth street church promptly tendered the use of their school-room for the purposes of the Centenary congregation; and on the following Sunday morning Mr. James Sullivan's society class met at the usual hour and held the first service after the fire in the new quarters.

The first public service was held in the church proper at half-past two o'clock, conducted by Rev. Mr. Sprague, who chose as his text Isaiah, xxvi., 4: "Trust ye in the Lord for ever; for in the Lord Jehovah is everlasting strength." In the evening the two congregations united in a service and were addressed by Rev. Joseph Hart, pastor of Exmouth street church, and Rev. H. Sprague.

It was a time in which the affairs of the community were altogether deranged and personal matters exacted close attention, yet the people were not so engrossed as to lose sight of the duty they owed to their church and consideration was early given to the matter of rebuilding. Some delay was occasioned by reason of the session of the conference which opened in the week after the fire. On the other hand, the early session of that body greatly facilitated building operations, because deputations were appointed by it to visit England, the United States and the provinces to solicit aid in the rebuilding of the churches. Conference being over a meeting of trustees was held on July 5th, when Mr. Sprague announced that he had been appointed the deputation to visit England, and that in his absence Rev. Joseph Hart would act as superintendent of the circuit. At this meeting a building committee, consisting of J. V. Troop, D. J. McLaughlin, G. Bent, C. W. Wetmore, A. L. Palmer, T. A. Temple and W. H. Tuck, was appointed. Subsequently Mr. Troop resigned and Captain Prichard was appointed in his place. The committee immediately entered upon its duties and recommended the purchase of more land. They were given power to act and purchased the lot on Princess street adjoining the church property on the west, at the price of $2,000; also, the Varley trust lots on Leinster street, as well as the lease of the McDade lot adjoining, paying, therefore, respectively $4,000 and $1,200. This transaction gave the trustees a property of 225 feet on Wentworth and 120 feet on Princess and Leinster streets. Plans were called for and those of Mr. John Welch, architect of New York, accepted. The work of building the school-room or vestry was immediatly undertaken, resulting in the handsome structure now used for that purpose.

Mr. Sprague was absent during the greater part of the summer. In the meantime services were of course held in Exmouth street, the two congregations uniting on sacramental occasions. The great Indian famine occurring in that year had aroused the sympathies of the English people, and the Wesleyans of England were engaged in a special effort in behalf of their own famine-stricken missions in that great country. Mr. Sprague's visit was, therefore, made at an unpropitious time, yet he was well received and in his mission successful in raising between sixteen and seventeen thousand dollars.

A fire occurring in Portland a few months after the great fire, destroyed the Methodist church and put another claimant upon the church relief fund. Upon the distribution of this fund, by the committee appointed by conference, the share allotted to Centenary was $9,286.

After Mr. Sprague's return from England the condition of his health was such as, in his opinion, to unfit him in a measure for the responsibilities that attach to church work of a circuit like Centenary. To his people his ministrations had been most satisfactory, and it was with deep concern that his quarterly board, in his second year, learned of the possibility of his accepting the invitation extended to him to become president of the Mount Allison college. They took early action; expressed great regret at his possible separation, and earnestly requested him, if he could deem it in the line of his duty, to remain another year. Having taken time to consider, Mr. Sprague, at the next meeting of the board, stated that his health had very greatly and encouragingly improved and he would have pleasure in accepting the invitation for the third year, upon the understanding that conference should be asked to appoint an assistant to him,— such arrangement not to involve additional expense upon the circuit. This being assented to the appointments were made, Rev. M. R. Knight coming as assistant.

On the 10th November, 1878, Mr. Sprague preached from Exodus, xxxiii., 15: "If thy presence go not with me, carry us not up hence." And on the following Sunday, the 17th November, the Sabbath school-room was opened. Rev. Joseph Hart, president of the conference, preached in the morning; Rev. John Allison addressed the Sabbath School in the afternoon, and Rev. William Mitchell preached in the evening.

Mr. Hart's subject was love for God's house, and based upon Psalms, xxiv., 8: "Lord, I have loved the habitation of thy house, and the place where thine honor dwelleth,"— being in part the inscription at the base of the large window in the school-room.

Mr. Allison's text in the afternoon was Exodus, ii., 9 : "And Pharaoh's daughter said unto her, take this child away, and nurse it for me, and I will give thee thy wages. And the woman took the child and nursed it."

Mr. Mitchell in the evening preached from Matthew, xii., 6 : " In this place is one greater than the temple."

On the following Sunday Rev. B. Chappell preached in the morning and the Rev. Dr. McDonald, missionary to Japan, in the evening. So that it was not until the third Sunday that our own pastor occupied the pulpit. On that day Rev. M. R. Knight preached in the morning and Rev. H. Sprague in the evening.

Rev. Joseph Hart succeeded Rev. Howard Sprague, having been appointed in 1879 upon the invitation of the quarterly board. The appointment almost came as a matter of course, because in addition to Mr. Hart's eminent qualifications for the position, he had for some time been very closely identified with the interests of Centenary congregation. His influence was an important factor in the selection of the church plans. The building of the school room was commenced under him while acting as superintendent in Mr. Sprague's absence, and the completion of the greater enterprize was his dream. It was with high hopes that he entered upon his ministry.

It was not long before he called a meeting of the congregation with a view of taking immediate action looking to the erection of the church proper according to the plans already prepared. He stated his own views and impressed upon the people what in his judgment was their duty. After an interchange of views a subscription was proposed which met with so hearty a response that the work seemed assured. Matters were about taking definite shape when it was observed that the ill health under which Mr. Hart had been suffering for some time, and which was not viewed with any apprehension of danger, was indeed of a very serious character. So anxious was he to see the work proceed that he bravely contended with his malady until physical strength became exhausted. On the first Sunday in November he preached his last sermon.

A quarterly meeting was held at the parsonage on the 12th December, 1879, presided over by Gilbert Bent until all matters of business had been dealt with. Mr. Hart then entered the room, and, according to the minutes of the Recording Steward, "Stated that the illness under which he had been for a long time suffering, and which had recently so completely prostrated him, he had lately discovered to be much more serious than he had supposed : so serious that he felt his work on earth to be over. He referred in very touching and impressive terms to the bright anticipations of usefulness which he had when appointed to Centenary circuit; anticipations not now to be realized, in the wise providence of God ; and feelingly spoke of the Divine consolations which he enjoyed in his present sore affliction, and of his hopeful anticipations of the end. He stated that he had made arrangements for the pulpit to be supplied for the remaining half of the year " (details of which are omitted). Proceeding with the record : "Without waiting for the formality of a resolution, the meeting with one voice heartily and affectionately accepted the proposals of Rev. Mr. Hart; tendering him their warmest sympathy in his affliction, and emphasizing their acceptance of any arrangement which he should find conducive to his comfort and welfare." Then retiring from the room visibly affected and in extreme weakness, Mr. Hart for the last time left his quarterly meeting. It was a touching scene, and one long to be remembered by those present.

During a long and painful illness Mr. Hart was indeed sustained by the Divine consolation of which he spoke. On the 19th of March, 1880, in the 46th year of his age and the 27th of his ministry, having "fought the good fight of faith," he entered into that rest that remaineth to the people of God.

The following resolutions, expressive of the church's grief at the loss of their pastor, were, at a meeting held on the 21st of March, read by A. A. Stockton, and, on motion of Captain Prichard, seconded by E. T. Knowles, adopted.

"The members of the quarterly board of the Centenary Methodist church in Saint John, receive with deepest sorrow the announcement of the death of their beloved pastor, the Reverend Joseph Hart, who, during the twenty-six years of faithful ministerial labor in connection with the Methodist church in these provinces, was distinguished for his scholarly attainments, his Christian deportment and his activity in the promotion of the social, moral and intellectual welfare of society.

"Firmly holding the doctrines of our church he sought by his preaching, which was earnest, thoughtful and persuasive, to incite his hearers to piety, purity of heart and holy living. Sedulous in the performance of his pastoral duties, tenderly sympathetic in his disposition, he was peculiarly qualified to administer consolation to the sick and troubled. His admirable executive abilities rendered him efficient in carrying forward church enterprises.

"We gratefully remember the kindly interest manifested by him in the work of this church and his supervision of it during the absence in England of the Rev. Howard Sprague and during the erection of the present school building. His intimate acquaintance with our affairs, acquired through this unofficial relationship well fitted him for the position afterwards assigned him by the conference as our pastor, and justified him in entertaining the high hopes with which he entered upon the performance of the duties of his pastorate ; be it therefore

Resolved, That we record our sense of the loss sustained by the Methodist Church of Canada, our missionary cause, our educational institutions and the New Brunswick and Prince Edward Island Conference, in common with the membership and congregation of the church, in the lamented death of the Reverend Joseph Hart, while yet in the prime of his manhood and his mental energy ; and, also, our grief at the severance of the many strong individual ties of friendship formed in the circuit in which he was called to labor ; and be it further

Resolved, That conscious of the anguish which must attend the deeper bereavement sustained by our pastor's widow, we tender to her our sincerest sympathy in this her severe affliction."

The quarterly board and board of trustees followed the mourners in the procession to the railway station, from whence the remains were taken to Halifax for interment.

Rev. John Prince having, at the request of Mr. Hart, already assumed the duties of superintendent of the circuit, continued to discharge them until the end of the term.

The trustee steward D. J. McLaughlin, Jr., having taken up his residence in another part of the province, tendered his resignation ; and on the 21st June, 1880, H. J. Thorne was elected to the position thus made vacant.

The position of the church now involved much responsibility and it was evident that Mr. Hart's successor should be a person distinguished for his executive ability and an administrator of experience. The reputation of Rev. D. D. Currie, at that time editor of the *Wesleyan*, seemed to point to him as a suitable supply, and on a majority vote an invitation was extended. The appointment was made and he entered upon his duties in July, 1880. Mr. Currie, finding plans prepared and a subscription list already opened, lost no time in getting at work. The subscription list was revised as to its conditions somewhat and appeared larger than that made in Mr. Hart's time, but there really was little difference between them. Twenty-five persons subscribed $12,900, being upwards of $500 on an average for each individual.

In August, upon the nomination of the superintendent, the

following persons were appointed trustees: H. B. White, L. H. Vaughan, E. Frost, W. H. Hayward and J. E. Irvine; and in September, Judge Palmer, T. A. Temple and W. H. Tuck were also appointed. Mr. Tuck declined to act, but the others assumed office.

CENTENARY CHURCH.

Tenders for building the church having been asked for, that of Messrs. Bond & Milden was accepted. The work was undertaken and the building opened on the 27th of August, 1882.

When the tower and spire are completed the cut above presented will correctly indicate the appearance of the church as it may be viewed from Princess street.

On the day of opening, long before the hour at which the service was to begin, the congregation began to assemble, and soon every seat was occupied. Chairs were placed in the aisles and gallery wherever it was possible. At 11 o'clock Rev. Messrs. Daniel, Narraway, Milligan, Pope, Lathern and Currie entered and took their places on the platform. Hymn 668 was sung, after which Rev. H. Daniel offered prayer. The *Te Deum* was then sung, followed by Scripture lessons prescribed by the liturgy and read by Rev. H. Pope, D. D., and Rev. Geo. S. Milligan, D. D. The congregation joined with the choir in singing the dedication hymn, No. 676,—

>Great King of Glory, come,
>And with Thy favour crown
>This temple as Thy home.
>This people as Thine own:
>Beneath this roof, Oh deign to show
>How God can dwell with men below.

Rev. Geo. Douglas, D. D., of Montreal, had been announced to preach the dedicatory sermon, but was taken ill on the journey to Saint John. In his absence the sermon was preached by Rev. J. Lathern, whose text was, "Now unto Him who is able to do exceeding abundantly above all that we ask or think according to the power that worketh in us, unto Him be glory in the church by Christ Jesus, throughout all ages, world without end. Amen."—Eph. iii., 20-21.

During the offertory the choir sang Gounod's fine anthem, "Send out Thy Light," and shortly afterwards the congregation united with them in singing hymn 675,—

>Lord of Hosts! to Thee we raise
>Here a house of prayer and praise:
>Thou Thy people's hearts prepare
>Here to meet for praise and prayer.

During the singing of this hymn the following trustees, Joseph Prichard, Geo. Thomas, Thomas A. Temple, Alfred A. Stockton, Henry J. Thorne, Gilbert Bent, Edward T. Knowles, Richard W. Thorne, William H. Hayward and Judge Palmer, going forward to the communion rail, the usual dedication service was proceeded with, Capt. Prichard, on behalf of the trustees, saying to the superintendent, "We present unto you this building, to be dedicated as a church for the worship and service of Almighty God." The congregation then standing, Mr. Currie repeated the usual declaration after which the service was brought to a close.

The members of the choir present at this service were: Miss Ennis, organist; J. Clawson, leader; soprano, Miss Ella Clawson, Miss Robinson, Mrs. H. J. Thorne, Miss White; alto, Miss Alice Hea, Miss Minnie Hea, Miss Hattie Prichard, Miss Annie Turner; tenor, Dr. Daniel, J. Clawson, F. McInnis, William Kain, James A. White; bass, H. B. White, Henry Turner, S. Kerr, J. McKillop, John S. Hale.

In the afternoon a Sabbath school service was held, presided over by Rev. Dr. Pope and addressed by the chairman and Rev. Messrs. Read, Shenton and W. W. Lodge.

In the evening Rev. D. D. Currie preached from 1 Kings, vi., 7, drawing appropriate lessons and making applications suggested by the passages in their reference to the building of Solomon's temple.

At the evening service Minnie Emily and Harry LeBaron, children of J. Albert Venning, received the rite of adult baptism, and Ethel Maud, infant daughter of E. V. Hunt, the rite of infant baptism.

William Kerley, who came recommended in the usual way from the M. E. Church of Ontario, as a local preacher of twenty-five years standing, and Mrs. Emma Kerley, his wife, who came recommended from the Methodist Church in Brantford, Ontario, were received into membership at this service.

The first church was opened on 16th August, 1839, being the centennial year of the founding of British Methodism. The second church was opened on 27th August, 1882, being the centennial year of Methodism in the Lower Provinces.

The building faces south on Princess street and displays on the front a surface of masonry 80 feet wide, with a total height to the top of the carved stone on the apex of the roof of 88 feet. A handsome Gothic door-way, flanked by stone columns with enriched capitals, approached by a flight of stone steps, is the main entrance to the sacred edifice.

The principal window, which is over the door way, is of large size, being 20 feet wide and 40 high, divided into seven lights of beautiful design. Heavy stone buttresses support the corners of the building, which are surmounted with massive pinacles. The tower is on the east side, about sixteen feet from the front, and is very imposing, spacious and richly ornamented, the angles being stayed by buttresses similar in character to those of the main building. The tower is 25 feet square at the base, and at present is built up 40 feet from the ground. A large Gothic door-way, 14 feet wide and 7 feet high on the east side, leads into the tower, which forms a handsome and spacious porch through which access is gained to the main building.

The Wentworth street elevation, extending north 116 feet, has six windows in the east aisle 7 by 22 feet and eight clerestory windows 7 by 12 feet, each divided into three lights and enriched with elegant tracery. The west side is designed and finished in the same way.

Besides the south and east doors, entrance is obtained to the church by a door at the south-west and two others at the northern end leading from the school room.

The clere-story is supported by massive iron columns, each 24 feet long and weighing 5,000 lbs. The capitals and bases are of moulded wood.

Immediately within the south porch is a vestibule extending the width of the nave and built up of ash. The northern side of the screen and the east and west doors are pierced with lancet lights, filled in with stained glass of chaste design, each light bearing a circular medallion of floral pattern, the interstices between the upper parts of the windows being filled with smaller medallions, each bearing the *fleur de lis*.

The roof, the apex of which is 65 feet above the floor, is painted a full sky blue, and the ground-work is in imitation of pitch pine, having at the intersections foliated bosses of lemon color, — a simple and pleasing combination of tints.

Some six feet from the front range of pews is the communion rail of black walnut carved in simple open-work design, and within which, set back four feet, is the platform, raised three feet above the floor level and extending the full width of the nave. The pulpit-desk and furniture are the gifts of the contractors; Miss Eaton presented the Bible and hymn book; the elegant altar is the gift of A. A. Stockton; the clock in the church was given by J. R. Ferguson; while the beautiful baptismal font was presented some time afterwards by the infant class of the Sabbath school.

The organ, which in part was new and in part the organ of the Mechanics' Institute, is very imposing in appearance, but disappointing and unsatisfactory in musical effect.

The most approved apparatus was provided for the lighting of the church, the principal fittings being two pendant sun-lights of large size, so arranged as to throw a soft and even light over the whole of the upper and centre part of the interior, and in the aisles under the galleries are arranged semi-circular coronals, each having six gas-lights. The whole of the gas-fittings, including those of the pulpit platform, are of polished brass. The large reflectors are of white porcelain highly polished. In late years, in view of some of the porcelain having fallen from its place, it was deemed advisable to introduce a system of net work to conserve the safety of the congregation.

The seating capacity is large, there being on the ground floor 140 pews and 92 in the galleries, providing sittings for about 1,400 persons. The pews, which have open ends, are constructed of ash, with mouldings of black walnut varnished.

The School Building, which is a continuation of the main church and appears externally as transepts to it, covers a plot of ground about 100 feet by 50 feet, and is of two stories, the lower floor being given to class-rooms, parlors, etc., all well lighted. A corridor extends the whole length of the inner side, with entrances at each end, having very liberal well-planned stairs in the extended building both front and rear, which form the ends of the aisles of the main church and are the rear access to its galleries.

The school and lecture room is on the upper floor and is its chief attraction, for although the building externally is very beautiful in its proportions and built entirely of stone of the neighborhood and commends itself to all beholders, the magnificent interior will stand as an example of the most beautiful era of Gothic architecture. On one side of the room are six three-light windows, and in each end are lofty four-light windows, with lancets on each side all filled with elaborate and massive stone tracery. The whole of the steep-pitched roof is made to appear internally, and is what is technically known as the "hammer-beam" mode of construction, all the massive timber work being wrought out of hard pine, the many spandrels being filled in with varying tracery work, with mouldings, battlements and enrichments. All the wood framed-work is oiled and finished in its natural colors, the intervening panels being finished of a brilliant blue with an ornamental border of white and red. The interior is about fifty-six feet in height to the ridge, and although the roof frame-work starts from the stone corbels ten feet from the floor, there is no tie or connexion across it below the collar-beam at the top, which gives to the whole a very airy and roomy appearance, though it is constructively sound and strong. One end of the lecture room is partitioned off by ornamental screen work, forming a library and a large separated infant-school room above, arranged to seat 200 children or 100 adults in an end gallery when the moveable screen work is opened. All the windows are filled with rich stained-glass, largely in geometric patterns. The principal four-light front window, with its side-lights, being made a specialty and superior to the rest, the large window having appropriate texts, surrounding rich foliage in medallion and the large foliated circle of its traceried head having an angel with a flowing scroll inscribed in latin, "Peace on earth," etc. The side or lancet windows — both memorial gifts — are beautiful specimens of artistic work in glass. One represents the nativity, with the wise men of the east offering their worship to the infant Saviour; it bears at the base the inscription "Presented by Henrietta Temple, A. D. 1878." The other shows our Saviour taking the little children in His arms and blessing them, and has the text, "Suffer little children to come unto me and forbid them not, for of such is the kingdom of heaven," and at the base the words, "In memoriam, Willie Welch, died 1868, aged 4 years."

The stone work of all the windows and finishings is artificial and was prepared by D. H. Wheeler. James Thompson was the mason; Herman Royeman did the frame work of the roof; and Purdy French the balance of the carpenter work.

During the interval between the destruction of the old church and the opening of the new the pilgrimage of some who had for years been familiar figures in the congregation was brought to a close. At the mention of the name of John

Gardiner many will call to mind a quiet, unobtrusive gentleman, a christian of deep and steadfast piety, the tenor of whose life was characterized by meekness and humility. He was the first superintendent of the Sabbath School, and during all the time of twenty years in which he filled that office it is said he missed but two sessions. Many who are now in the congregation remember him well as their Sabbath School superintendent and will quickly accord to him the respect to which his name is entitled. Mr. Gardiner died in the month of February, 1878.

In the same month the death of William Whiteside took place. He was a brother-in-law of Mr. Gardiner, and before the erection of the first church and for many years after that date had been an active member of the Methodist Society, and an efficient local preacher. In later years he was not active, but for some time before his death was in the enjoyment of that religion which brings to its possessor so much joy and peace.

The death of Henry Whiteside occurred on May 3, 1879. He was a person whose "face illumined" seemed to indicate that he had reached mountain peaks of christian satisfaction. Out of the abundance of his heart his mouth did speak, sometimes in a sudden, joyous, ejaculation, "glory!" that to the stranger who might be near him produced a sensation quite startling; at other times, as opportunity offered, in the social services, on the street, or at his place of employment, bearing testimony to the love of God that was in his heart. Quick to recognize his own duty, he was not slow in indicating to others what he conceived to be theirs; particularly would this be the case if the week-night service was a little dull.

Henry and William were sons of Richard Whiteside, who was Recording Steward of the Circuit for so many years. Mrs. Barrett and Mrs. McCarty, wives of two worthy and respected Methodist ministers, were also of Richard Whiteside's family, and are at present members of and worshippers in Centenary church.

On October 2, 1881, Jacob V. Troop died. Mr. Troop had been connected with Centenary Church almost from the opening. In the early years, as already stated, he was a member of the choir and also an officer in the Sabbath School. For a number of years he had been a trustee and was secretary of the Varley Trust, in the purposes of which he was deeply interested. He served faithfully and well as an official in the church of which for many years he was a member, and was useful and respected as a citizen. He had much strength of purpose and force of character and withal the courage of his convictions. While not ostentatious in his liberality, he contributed largely toward the support of the church with which he was indentified and to such other interests as merited assistance. At the time of his death he was seventy-two years of age.

John Jenkins, an Englishman, born in June, 1812, was a resident of St. John for many years and died in October, 1882. For a long time he was connected with Centenary church, was a class leader and for some years assistant to Mr. Gardiner, as superintendent of the Sabbath school, in which position he was efficient and deeply interested. At a time when there were many prominent workers, he was one of the foremost, and by his extraordinary gifts in prayer and fervency in exhortation added much interest to the social services. In the late years of his life he was much missed in those services, his absence from them no doubt being largely due to physical infirmities. While feeling himself obliged to withdraw from active work in the church, yet by precept and example in the home circle he exercised an influence that is now manifest in the lives of his children.

Dennis Sullivan was permitted to see the opening of the new church and to join in those exercises, but it was not long before he was visited by a sickness that resulted in his death on the 6th December, 1882, in the sixty-ninth year of his age. He was a very worthy member both of the church with which he was connected and the community in which he lived. He was respected by all persons whose opinion was of any value. His piety was deep and uniform, and from the commencement to the close of his christian pilgrimage he walked worthy of his religious profession. His religion was exhibited in his daily intercourse with society and by his unfeigned faith and godly sincerity. As a local preacher he was always at his post and ministered to the people with much acceptance. He was ever ready to take part in the social services of the church, and in the class-meeting was sympathetic, helpful and interesting. In taking one of his last appointments as a local preacher, he was thrown from his carriage, in consequence of the horse running away, and sustained injuries from which probably he never recovered. While this accident was not the immediate cause of his death yet no doubt it greatly aggravated the illness which closed his exemplary and religious life.

There are many others of whom mention should have been made in chronological order, who years before the destruction of the old church had passed from it, either by reason of death or of their removal to other scenes of christian labor. Those removed by death were Johnston Sullivan, Isaac Johnston, Frederick Harrison, James M. Hamilton, George M. Dixon, Sampson Manaton and others, who after lives of great usefulness passed to their reward. Among those who left St. John, forming elsewhere home and church ties, were Peter LeSueur, Edward Lloyd, Henry Marshall, Robert Hannah, John McMoran, William Warwick and many others.

It will be seen that the personal references in the previous pages have been to official members. This statement will serve as an explanation for the omission of names that may have been looked for—names of persons well reported for good works, who, though not officially connected with the church, yet exercised an influence by their piety and usefulness that will be understood only in the great revealing day. To attempt to do otherwise than has been undertaken would obviously be both incomplete and unsatisfactory. For this reason, also, little has been said of the godly women of the church, of whom there were not a few—mothers in Israel, who were "full of good works and alms-deeds which they did," given to hospitality,—whose efforts in many instances were characterized by as much if not more zeal and earnestness than distinguished the husbands whose names have received mention. Among very successful and intelligent class leaders and earnest christian workers should be mentioned Mrs. Richard Whiteside, Mrs. Hutchings, Mrs. Drury, Mrs. Chamberlain, Mrs. Hennigar, Mrs. Johnston, Mrs. McCallum, and Mrs. Henry Whiteside. Mrs. Hutchings is still connected with the church, but age and infirmities have long deprived her of its privileges. Mrs. McCallum some times visits the city and invariably is found in the church services. Of the others, some have removed, and the rest are among the redeemed in heaven. In addition to these there were some who, while active in the old church, continued their labors in the new, and were of great blessing to many who came within their influence.

In November following the opening exercises the pulpit in the new church was for the first time occupied by one of our General Superintendents, S. D. Rice, D. D., who preached from Heb. xi., 26. It will be remembered that Dr. Rice, in the early years of Centenary Church, labored in St. John, and was held in high esteem. During the long time in which the preacher had been separated from the friends of his early ministry many changes had taken place, and the few who remained appreciated the privilege of listening to one for whom they had so much respect, and of renewing an acquaintance happily formed so many years before.

Early in 1883 the question of union of all the Methodist bodies in Canada greatly agitated the society throughout the Dominion. A very strong feeling against the proposal existed in the minds of many of our ministers, while the laymen were pronounced in its favor. On 12th of February a meeting of officials in connection with the St. John Circuits was held in the Centenary, and, upon a vote being taken, seventy-two voted in favor and one against the proposed basis of union. In the following March, at a meeting of the Quarterly Board, the vote stood 23 to 2.

Great preparations had been made for the celebrating, on the 18th May, 1883, the Centennial of the landing of the Loyalists. It was deemed fitting that the second century should be ushered in by a watch-night service to be held in Centenary Church on the evening of the 17th May. That service was accordingly held and attended by an immense gathering. All the aisles and corridors were packed, and the greatest enthusiasm prevailed. Of this service Dr. Elder, in an editorial in the *Daily Telegraph*, wrote: "The evening meeting in the beautiful Centenary Church was happily conceived and well carried out. The presence of the Lieutenant Governor, Hon. R. D. Wilmot; Chief Justice Allen; American Consul, Gen. Warner; Mayor Jones; J. W. Lawrence, Esq., and many of our most prominent clergymen and laymen, and of an overflowing and deeply interested audience, made the occasion one of deep interest. Music and sacred song, solemn addresses, and eloquent speech, the teachings of history and the sanctions of religion, were all successfully invoked to make the occasion forever memorable." When the closing hour of the first century struck, the vast audience arose, and the grand strains of Old Hundred, sung by almost two thousand voices, rang through the lofty arches of the church. Rev. Mr. Daniel then pronounced the benediction, and the great gathering dispersed after singing "God Save the Queen."

As an incident to the Loyalist celebration, on the third of the following October, a Literary and Musical Centennial Harvest Festival in aid of tree planting was held in the Centenary Church, the Lieutenant Governor being in the chair, besides whom there were on the platform the United States Consul, Chief Justice Allen, Hon. S. L. Tilley, C. B., Rev. Messrs. Dobson, Currie, and others.

In the erection of the church it would not be right, nor is there any disposition, to withhold from Rev. D. D. Currie the credit that is due him for the assiduity with which he attended to details incident to that enterprise. In his board of trustees, however, he had a band of busy men willing to undertake the responsibility that attached to their office. It would be invidious to make distinction. Some may have accomplished more than others, but all were disposed to do their utmost, and to them as a body the congregation accord much credit.

Stained glass windows representing miracles and parables of our Lord have been placed in position. Some were put in during Mr. Currie's pastorate and the others in Mr. Dobson's. They were supplied by J. C. Spence & Son of Montreal, and are creditable to the skill of the manufacturer, being pleasing in appearance and effective in design. Seven are in memory of friends, while two are simply presentation windows. The memorial class were placed to the memory of Rev. Joseph Hart, representing the parable of the sower; Jacob V. Troop, the miracle of Christ stilling the tempest; Mr. and Mrs. Aaron Eaton, the feeding of the five thousand; Mrs. A. L. Palmer, parable of the lost sheep; Mr. and Mrs. John Frost, the miraculous draught of fishes; Mrs. George Thomas, parable of the good Samaritan; Mrs. Eliza Kennay Smith, the raising of the daughter of Jairus. The others were presented by Miss Troop, representing the parable of the laborers in the vineyard; and Mr. E. R. Moore, representing the marriage in Cana.

On June 1st, 1883, Henry J. Thorne having resigned the position of trustee steward, George A. Henderson was appointed to that office, and entering upon his duties has discharged them ever since.

With the Conference of 1883 Mr. Currie's ministerial term expired. An invitation was extended to Rev. William Dobson and the appointment was made. Mr. Dobson entered upon his work on July 22, preaching from Acts iv., 13, "And they took knowledge of them that they had been with Jesus." The large congregations he had during the three years in which he ministered to the people showed the popularity in which as a preacher he was held. Under him the collections increased and the pew rent roll was augmented by upwards of three hundred dollars. There were additions to the membership, and in every department the interest was so well sustained that it may be said his term was one of success.

The Conference of 1884, by invitation previously extended, was held in Centenary Church. This is known as the "Long Conference," as it involved the completion of all business of the annual Conference in connection with the Methodist Church of Canada, and in accordance with the terms of union, the organization of the Conference in connection with the Methodist Church. At the latter Conference Rev. Dr. Williams presided.

In Mr. Dobson's term the congregation had the pleasure of listening to a number of distinguished preachers, among whom were Dr. Parker, of New York, Dr. Meacham, Dr. Williams, and Dr. Carman; and in January, 1885, Joseph Cook visited the city and lectured to large audiences in the Centenary

Church, his subjects being "Seven Modern Wonders of the World" and "Does Death End All."

On the 17th February, 1885, David Collins passed to his reward, in the eighty-sixth year of his age. Mr. Collins, at the time of his death, was a member of Exmouth street Church, but inasmuch as he was one of the original trustees of Centenary, and moreover a Christian who confined not his attentions to any one particular church, but was found wherever he might be useful, it is not out of place that in a record of this kind his name should receive mention. The first place among Methodists in St. John during a useful life of more than half a century is conceded to David Collins. He was warmly attached to the church of his choice. His experience was rich in spiritual enjoyment that was born within the veil. The light of his life did shine before men, and withal, his habitual modesty and deep humility gave to his other excellencies an added lustre. "His spirit and temper were such as became the gospel of Christ, and he departed in peace and holy hope, full of days and full of honor."

In the following month, March, 1885, the exemplary life of Ellen Barry Smith closed at the age of seventy-three. She was the daughter of Robert Barry, one of the earliest and most prominent members of the Methodist Society in Nova Scotia, niece of Rev. William Jessop, the noble pioneer of whom mention has been made as one of the early missionaries to Saint John; and the wife of Rev. William Smith, a faithful Methodist minister, to whom, by actively engaging in the duties of a minister's wife, she had been a great help. Becoming a widow in 1863, for a time she resided in Liverpool, but between that event and her death the greater portion of her life was spent in St. John, where she was earnest in her Master's cause. She was gifted to an unusual degree, powerful in prayer, persuasive in exhortation, and as a class leader earnest, sympathetic and intelligent. She sustained with wisdom her exalted Christian profession, and of her it may be said that religion regulated her understanding and her heart.

About this time a Missionary Committee was appointed by the Quarterly Board, of which James S. Marnie was secretary. As a result of this organization, and largely through the diligence of Mr. Marnie, the contributions of the congregation to the funds of the Society were very largely increased, until in a few years the amount contributed annually was double that of any year previous to the appointment of the committee.

A Woman's Missionary Society was also formed, the results of which have been most widespread. An account of this organization was prepared by a committee appointed for that purpose for the Jubilee record, and may properly be here presented.

WOMAN'S MISSIONARY SOCIETY.

In the year 1885 an Auxiliary to the Woman's Missionary Society was formed in connection with Centenary Church. Miss Hattie E. Smith, now Mrs. Eaton, of Baltimore, was its first president, and to her untiring exertions and judicious management much of its early success was owing.

The work of the New Brunswick and Prince Edward Island Branch, to which this Centenary Auxiliary belongs, was at first limited to Japan, but its contributions now augment the funds of the General Society. Under its present efficient head, Mrs. C. E. Macmichael, the work is growing and strengthening. Miss Palmer, its devoted corresponding secretary, has been wonderfully successful in awakening and directing missionary zeal among the women of our highly favored Methodism, and during the past year twenty-eight additional Auxiliaries have been formed. From these, representatives are sent to the annual meeting of the Branch.

The meetings of the Centenary Auxiliary, of which, also, Mrs. Macmichael is president, are held once a month, and have been made interesting from time to time by the reading of original papers and leaflets bearing on the work of Christian missions, as well as by letters received from the various fields to which grants are given. These extend from Japan to Newfoundland, and include the Girl's School at Tokio, the Crosby Girls' Home at Fort Simpson, the McDougall Orphanage, the Home at Chillewhack, the French work in Montreal, the Chinese Rescue Home in British Columbia, and an Orphanage for the children of fishermen in Newfoundland.

On November 15th, 1887, a Band was formed in connection with Centenary Auxiliary which has since been doing excellent work. It is known as the Haraiwa Mission Band. Miss Kate Bartlett was its first president. The well-known monthly periodical, the *Missionary Review*, is taken by the Auxiliary and circulated among its members, while one hundred and sixty copies of *The Outlook* find their way into the homes of the people through the agency of the Sabbath School. Last year, on the Friday of the week appointed for prayer by the Evangelical Alliance, a union meeting of the city Auxiliaries was held, and an Easter service has since been inaugurated which it is proposed to make an annual representative gathering, in the belief that there is no more fitting time for woman's combined and consecrated effort than the time which commemorates her heart-cheering commission, "Go your way; tell his disciples and Peter that he goeth before you into Galilee."

Mr. Dobson having reached the close of his pastorate, the Quarterly Board, at a meeting held in June, 1886, recorded its "high appreciation of his faithful services and of his able and fearless presentation of the truth to the congregation."

A call was extended to Rev. W. W. Brewer, and he succeeded Mr. Dobson, beginning his ministry in July, 1886. Mr. Brewer's public ministrations were marked by great earnestness and fervor, and as a messenger of Christ it was his endeavor to persuade men by gospel messages clearly and lovingly given. Under him an interesting and useful paper called *Glad Tidings* was published and received with favor. In his term much evangelistic effort was put forth through what was known as Band Work, and so far as that work was directed in the Lower Provinces he was the superintendent. He was also deeply interested in the outcasts and abandoned, many of whom received a great deal of care and attention at his hands. The extra work thus outlined, added to his circuit duties, represented an amount of labor that few men having respect for their health and strength would dare undertake.

During Mr. Brewer's pastorate, among distinguished preachers occupying the pulpit may be mentioned Rev. E. A. Telfer, whose sermon on the "Blessed South Wind" is well remembered; Rev. T. Bowman Stephenson, D. D.; Father Chiniquy; Mark Guy Pearse, who held a series of four Bible readings; Dr. Williams; Dr. Carman; Bishop Tanner, A. M. E. Church; Dr. Lowery; D. Savage; Bishop Foster, of the M. E. Church; and E. Hartley Dewart, D. D.

During his pastorate the ladies of the different Methodist Churches of the city formed a Sustentation Society, the object of which is to augment the receipts of ministers upon the dependant circuits of the N. B. and P. E. I. Conference. This is not peculiarly an institution of Centenary Church, but inasmuch as its membership is largely made up of the members and adherents of that church, was organized within its parlors, in which the regular meetings are still held, and receives a great deal of sympathy from the congregation, it should be ranked as an incident calling for notice. The members of this society are much interested in their work, and during its existence have, by their contributions and influence, done much to help the funds of the Sustentation movement.

One of the newspapers found in the box which had been placed in the corner stone of old Centenary contains an account of the celebration, on June 21st, 1838, of the Queen's coronation. Some extracts from it may be interesting, and in view of the next item in this history to receive notice, are here presented: "Business was laid aside, stores and shops closed, and as the day advanced multitudes of well-dressed people were promenading the streets and visiting those parts of the city where the oxen, which had been provided by the corporation, were in preparation for a public feast." * * * "Each was trying to outdo his fellow in display, and hundreds were catching a partial glimpse of the loyal and patriotic acts that were flitting before and about them. Thus the time rapidly passed until the hour of eleven, the time *when divine service commenced in the Wesleyan Chapel.* To many persons King and Queen Squares held forth great attractions — the roast beef and puddings of old England were shortly to be forthcoming." * * * "Then the barracks: there the military corps, the Royal Artillery and the gallant Eleventh were to perform their evolutions on their square; and those who were more seriously disposed could enter into the sanctuary and offer up their petitions for the happiness and prosperity of the reign they were then engaged in celebrating." The words in italics are not so printed in the newspaper from which the extract is taken.

There is also in the same paper an account of the Temperance Soiree or Convention held in the Wesleyan Sabbath School room, in celebration of the Queen's coronation. This festive gathering — the first of its kind — seems to have been very social and was marked by great enthusiasm. Rev. B. G. Gray, president of the temperance society, presided. "Addresses were delivered by the chairman, His Honor Mr. Justice Parker, Rev. Mr. Bamford, His Honor Neville Parker, and Dr. Bayard (Samuel). Tea and coffee, with suitable accompaniments, were served up in due order. At intervals was heard the soft strains of beguiling harmony blending in unison with some delightful words for the occasion. * * * The rich and the honorable conducted themselves alike to all; the hoary head and the wintry-white locks held unrestrained intercourse with the bloom of youth, male and female being promiscuously intermingled throughout. Then was manifested all that true disinterested adherence to British rule that the heart could long for or the Sovereign Queen desire. 'Bless God for such meetings, such government as this,' said a rev. gentleman present in the height of his enthusiasm; 'I spilt my blood for this government, and would do it again; and you, daughters,' said he, smiling on the youthful glow of female loveliness that surrounded him, 'you, daughters, would bind up the wounds.'" When one has heard of the eccentric and loyal Stephen Bamford, and of the pride with which he referred to his battle wounds, it is not difficult to identify the reverend gentleman. The account concludes " LONG LIVE VICTORIA REGINA, PATRONESS OF THE TEMPERANCE SOCIETIES —long may she reign!!"

We conclude, then, that the gathering in the old Germain Street Church was the only religious public gathering held in St. John upon the occasion referred to. There "the seriously disposed offered up their petitions for the happiness and prosperity of the reign they were engaged in celebrating."

We reverence the people who, while they had hearty sympathy with all that was good in the general rejoicing, and no doubt entered heartily into the plaudits and acclamation of the people, yet also recognized the propriety of betaking themselves to the house of God and invoking His blessing upon the young Queen.

When Her Most Gracious Majesty had reigned fifty years her loyal subjects throughout the vast empire entered with great enthusiasm into the proper celebration of her Jubilee.

On June 19, 1887, Jubilee Sunday, a commemorative religious service was held in Centenary Church, when the St. John Fusiliers in full force attended. The congregation numbered over two thousand persons. As the battalion filed into their places the organist played Viviani's celebrated " March of the Silver Trumpets," ending with " Harmony in the Dome," by the same composer. The battalion colors were placed near the preacher's desk. The services began by singing hymn 902, a prayer for the Queen :

O King of Kings, thy blessing shed
On our annointed Sovereign's head !
And, looking from thy holy heaven,
Protect the crown thyself hast given.

In this, as in other hymns, the organ and choir were accompanied by the Battalion Band. Rev. Dr. Pope led in prayer and read the Scripture lessons. The preacher on the occasion was the Rev. John Lathern, D. D., who chose as his text Rev., viii., 3, 4, 5.

In the afternoon there was a Jubilee Union Sunday School Service, the body of the church being occupied by the schools in connection with the Methodist churches of the City and Portland, while the galleries were packed by parents and friends of the scholars. His Worship Mayor Thorne, an official of the church, occupied the chair, and on the platform were Rev. Dr. Lathern, Rev. J. W. Wadman, Rev. D. D. Moore, J. W. Lawrence, Esq., and Henry Melick, Esq. Addresses were delivered by the chairman, J. W. Lawrence, Dr. Lathern, and

Rev. J. W. Wadman. There were also exercises in which members of the schools took part.

In the summer of 1887 the St. John Oratorio Society obtained the use of the church for the purpose of rendering Haydn's sacred musical composition "The Creation" and Mendolssohn's "St. Paul." On the 25th and 26th July large audiences listened with great delight to the performers, who were accompanied by the usual instruments. These were the first complete oratorios rendered in a church in St. John, and those who appreciate music of that character heard it then under the most favorable circumstances. The acoustics of the auditorium proved excellent for the purposes and owing to the sacred relations in which the people found themselves, the narrative was given complete without being broken by bursts of applause; moreover, in a church it would seem that the words are received with deeper reverence than in the ordinary concert hall.

In every year the messenger of death comes to the congregation and levies tribute; nor was there in Mr. Brewer's pastorate immunity from his visits. Early in the morning of Ash Wednesday in 1887, Feb. 23, the message came to Edward T. Knowles announcing that the hour of his departure was at hand. To his friends the summons was not unexpected, as for a long time his health had been feeble, and he had reached the advanced age of eighty-three years. He had lived in the sunlight of God's love, and was indeed as ripened grain ready to be garnered. Mr. Knowles was born in Nova Scotia, but the greater portion of his life had been spent in St. John, where he was much respected for his sterling qualities. One of the original trustees of Centenary Church, he outlived them all, and as an official in connection with Methodism he was one of the oldest in the city. He had an abiding interest in the church, and in the many positions to which he was appointed or elected he served faithfully and well. A few days after his death the Quarterly Board placed on record the following resolution: "Whereas, since our last quarterly meeting, it has pleased Almighty God to remove from our society our brother Edward T. Knowles, who for almost half a century has been an official in connection with this church; and, whereas, this Board has the most pleasing recollections of his services, both in his official and society relations; therefore resolved, that we record our profound respect for his memory, and extend to his family our sympathy in their affliction."

To George Thomas the messenger came much more swiftly. Though he had for a long time been in poor health, yet his death took place when it was not looked for. Mr. Thomas had been a familiar figure in Centenary Church, and until within a few years of his death was an active and interested member in its general work. He had also been a trustee for some years, and gave close and intelligent attention to the duties incident to that office. He was painstaking and methodical in all that he did, conservative in his views, and firm, it' may be said, in his conservatism. These qualities, exhibited in his church relations, at times proved to be of great advantage in the administration of its affairs. He was deeply interested in the Varley trust, and was absent from the meetings of that board only when his health or other just reason prevented his attendance. His death took place on the 27th of April, 1888, in the seventy-ninth year of his age. Mr. Thomas was a native of Nova Scotia, and came from that part of the province which had also given to Centenary Messrs. Eaton, Ray, Knowles, Troop, Bent, and others.

The last name to be noticed in Mr. Brewer's pastorate is that of James Emison, a gentleman of kind and trusting disposition, of whom no one knew anything discreditable. At the time of the fire he had been for many years an efficient class leader; after that event he met in class while his health permitted, but did not act as leader. He was pre-eminently a man of faith and prayer, and his sincerity was manifested by the intensity, earnestness and simplicity with which he approached the throne of grace. Few men in the church, perhaps none, experienced more satisfaction in the religion of Christ. Though his hearing was impaired and he was largely shut out from the harmony of sound, yet he was regular in his attendance upon the public services, and it was evident that he had a very rich Christian experience which deepened and matured as he approached the end of his pilgrimage. There was no darkness in the valley as he passed through it, but with him "at evening time it was light," and "the Lord his God gave him rest," on the 17th January, 1889, in the eighty-sixth year of his age.

Centenary is now approaching its jubilee, and as a suitable introduction to the observance of that event the session of the Conference of 1889 was, by invitation, held within its walls. With this Conference Mr. Brewer's term expired. From one reason and another, principally from the fact of it being what was termed an off year, considerable difficulty was experienced in securing supply for the next year. The Stationing Committee had a good many sessions, and expressed anxiety to meet the wishes of the Quarterly Board as communicated to them through a committee appointed for that purpose. With each proposition it would seem that some interest was invaded, and the disposition of the matter involved much wisdom. It was not until after the Conference adjourned that the matter was finally disposed of by the special committee in the appointment of Rev. Edwin Evans, who, as the jubilee exercises approached, had ministered to the people for a few weeks.

THE JUBILEE.

In the growth of a community, as well as in the life of an individual, interesting points are reached when for a short time a halt is called and a glance both retrospective and prospective taken. None the less is it proper that a church should duly observe such periods in its history, giving praise for achievements, expressing sorrow for failures, and in each case carefully observing the lessons suggested with a view to the profitable application of the same in the years yet to come. Such a point had now been reached in the history of Centenary Church, and with a view to the appropriate observance of its jubilee the following programme, prepared by a joint committe of the Trustee and Quarterly Boards, was carried out:

August 18th, Sunday.
11.00 a. m., ... Rev. William Dobson
2.30 p. m., ... Sabbath School Service
7.00 p. m., ... Rev. H. Sprague, D. D.

August 19th, Monday, 8 p. m.
A Glance at Methodism, as it Was and as it Is.

August 20th, Tuesday, 8 p. m.
Reminiscences.

August 21st, Wednesday, 8 p. m.
Love Feast.

August 22nd, Thursday, 8 p. m.
Social Reunion,
A feature of which will be a Musical Programme by present and past Members of Choir.

August 23rd, Friday, 8 p. m.
Unveiling of Tablet, Historical Abstract, Etc.

August 25th, Sunday, 11 a. m. and 7 p. m.
John P. Newman, D. D.,
Bishop of M. E. Church of the United States.

August 26th, Monday, 8 p. m.
Lecture by Bishop Newman. Subject: "March of Civilization."

As the Sundays of 1889 fell upon the same days of the month as in 1839, it followed that Jubilee Sunday was exactly the 50th anniversary. The church was made attractive by floral decorations, and, as a feature both appropriate and interesting, around the galleries were hung portraits, chiefly in oil, of gentlemen who in years past took a warm interest in the church's welfare. The eastern gallery was adorned with paintings of John Gardiner, Aaron Eaton, J. V. Troop, D. J. McLaughlin, Senior, and Jeremiah Gove, while on the western gallery there were those of Gilbert T. Ray, George King, Thomas Hutchings, and John McAlpine. Over the altar and in front of the pulpit a fine portrait of Dr. Richey was placed, and on the northern end, under the gallery, were to be seen smaller portraits of that gentleman and of Dr. Alder, as well as an excellent picture of Centenary Church as it was. It will be remembered that Dr. Richey and Dr. Alder preached the dedicatory sermons in 1839. In the choir gallery were placed portraits of Rev. William Temple, a former superintendent of the circuit, and Rev. Dr. Punshon, who on several occasions in the old church had, by his wonderful oratory, delighted the multitudes, while over and above them all was to be seen the well-known picture of the founder of the Methodist Society, the beloved John Wesley. The eleven o'clock service was opened by the singing of Hymn 24:

> Holy, holy, holy, Lord God Almighty!
> Gratefully adoring our song shall rise to Thee;
> Holy, holy, holy, merciful and mighty,
> God in three persons, blessed Trinity.

Prayer was then offered by Rev. J. R. Narraway, followed by the singing of the Te Deum by the choir. The first lesson from Leviticus xxx., 8, was read by Rev. Wm. Dobson. The choir then rendered the first chant:

> O come, let us sing unto the Lord!

after which Mr. Dobson read the second lesson—Ephesians, third chapter, being the chapter in which the first text preached from in the old church was found. This fact was referred to by the reader as he approached the text.

After singing hymn 211,—

"Blow ye the trumpet, blow.
. . . . .
The year of Jubilee is come:
Return, ye ransom'd sinners, home!"

Mr. Dobson, the preacher of the occasion, announced as his text Leviticus xxv., 10: "And ye shall hallow the fiftieth year, and proclaim liberty throughout all the land unto all the inhabitants thereof: it shall be a jubilee unto you; and ye shall return every man unto his possession, and ye shall return every man unto his family." The synoptic report published in the *Daily Telegraph* on Monday was as follows:

"In prefacing his sermon, the reverend gentleman said that the whole Hebrew dispensation was typical and emblematical of things unseen and eternal. The journey of the Israelites through Egypt and into the promised land of Canaan was figurative of the bondage of sin, the Christian's entry into eternal life, and a better knowledge of heavenly things. The authority vested in the Jewish chief priest was but typical of the power held in the Christian's high priest, the Saviour, the Lamb of God, the pure and exalted One that taketh away the sins of the world. 'Thus,' said the preacher, as Campbell said, 'have coming events cast their shadows before.'

"Among the Jewish political institutions, not the least in importance was their year of jubilee. This jubilee year derived its significance from the fact that it was instituted to warn or restrain the tendency of the human heart to acquire property unduly, which evil, even in these days, has been the cause of creating many monopolies which have been but the forerunners of much unhappiness. It was also intended to restrain any feeling of lording over weaker brethren, and, as far as possible, to destroy the perpetuity of slavery in the land. In that year every man who had forfeited his liberty became a free citizen. Yesterday but a slave, to-day he becomes a free man. In every heart is implanted a love of the land of birth. Nowhere, perhaps, is the feeling more hallowed than in the rural districts. To persons born under such circumstances it makes the heart ache to see the old homestead, where the mother had nursed the children in infancy, and the father tilled the land, pass into the hands of strangers. All these old associations fill the breast of the Hebrew slave who had forfeited his liberty; therefore to him the jubilee year was an important institution, inasmuch as it made him a free man.

"This is but typical of the moral and spiritual freedom which is promised to all those who obey the dictates of conscience. Moral freedom consists in the right to manifest all our nature without any restraint, for where there is any repression there is slavery. There are very few Christians, if any, whose natures are free in the proper sense of the word. The reasons for these are two-fold: First, there are very few who carry about with them a nature that can be manifested, at all times and under all conditions, in its fulness, without being restrained by what is called conscience; second, there are very few men who possess such a nature that they can manifest it in its entirety without finding themselves enslaved by God's law. Conscience is a something which is of itself undefinable, but it is possessed by every human being, and can never be utterly destroyed or annihilated. It assumes to itself the right to challenge every individual's actions and to determine their moral quality. This it does by pressing home upon all the moral character of their thoughts and actions. After a day of active work many a man has been brought face to face by conscience with the effect of his actions, been charged with unmanliness of action which he dared not contradict. This is the experience of all; therefore all are the slaves, more or less, of conscience. If, therefore, as is proved, moral freedom be the right to manifest all parts of nature without any restraint whatever, then all, to a certain extent, are the slaves of conscience. Why? Because they fear the lashes which it brings down upon them. They feel that down in the depths of their nature are elements so opposed to conscience that if they were allowed to manifest them in their fulness they must break not only the civil but God's law.

Hence they curtail the attributes of their nature and become slaves to the moral law. The only way men can become free is to be brought into harmony with conscience and God's moral law. This can only be done by the annihilation of certain parts of the nature. In order to make a successful voyage of life all men must be obedient to the commands of one supreme head. This supreme being is found in the Saviour. His commands must be obeyed, else, like the crew who, on shipboard, refuse to carry out the orders of the captain, there will be mutiny and rebellion. Every living being knows he or she was born for the enjoyment of higher and nobler things than they are now enjoying, viz., to become heirs with God and joint heirs with Christ, possessors of an inheritance which is incorruptible and fadeth not away. Hence Christ's commands must be obeyed, and his plan of redemption must be accepted. It is said that Whitfield prayed until his face grew radiant with the glory of God and his heart went out in love to Jesus and God, and that he loved his neighbor as himself. This experience of Whitfield's may become the possession of every member of the human family, for love of God and acceptance of Christianity will bring man in accord with the moral law, and make him the possessor of eternal inheritance.

"The preacher then closed with a few words to the members of the church, expressing the hope that the celebration of their 50th anniversary would fill them with increased energy and determination to work more earnestly for God and hasten forward the coming of Christ's kingdom."

SABBATH SCHOOL SERVICE.

The cradle of the church and the nursery from which the plants are brought is the Sabbath School. Perhaps in no department of church work is there more success accomplished than through the well directed efforts of the faithful Sabbath school teacher. It was therefore very fitting that upon so historic an occasion as that through which the church was now passing a special service should be held.

At this service, Miss Sarah E. Smith, one of the lady teachers, read the following original poem, appropriate to the occasion, entitled

OUR JUBILEE.

In the sweet story, often read,
    Amid the signs and wonders wrought of old,
A chosen people, through the desert led,
    Battling with doubts and dangers manifold,
Came, safe at last, to claim with thankful tears,
The long sought heritage of forty years!

Shall we, whose story is so like their own,
    Who fifty years of strange deliverance see,
To whose weak faith such wonders have been shown,
    Shall we not celebrate our jubilee?
And shall not in His ear our song be loud
Who leads His people still by fire and cloud?

We may not count the mercies of the way,
    Nor all the windings of the path explain,
We only know the darkness turned to day,
    And where the grief had been was joy again,
Up from the ashes of our buried past
Rose a new life and larger faith at last.

To-day we stand, unshod, with reverent feet,
    And gaze adown the vista of the years.
What miracles of change these years repeat,
    What growth of science, unforetold of seers,
What giant schemes, what vast designs have birth,
What searching of the secrets of the earth?

And in the realm of spirit, subtler far,
    How holy and how grand the triumphs won,
Even as in worth a soul transcends a star,
    And shall outshine in heaven the latest sun,
So our high boast such victories shall be
For these we celebrate our jubilee!

We welcome you to-day whose tearful thought
    Goes back in yearning to the long ago,
Past all the burdens which the years have brought,
    To kindle once again youth's fervid glow.
And people with the vanished forms of yore
The places which shall know them never more.

Perchance when first the sacred Temple rose,
   And altar fires ascended to the skies,
In your child hearts was sown the seed that grows
   And blossoms into noblest destinies.
And from your lips the same sweet lessons given
Led other souls to happiness and heaven.

Rejoice, rejoice that ye were counted meet,
   No worthier service could ye do or ask,
Fain would we follow where your willing feet
   Were swift to enter on the holy task;
We hail you pioneers upon the road,
White is the harvest from the seed you sowed!

And for the dead—for those who, one by one
   Fell wearied with the march beside the way,
Their tired hands folded, and their toil all done,
   Tender and sweet the memories to-day;
And grateful thanks for all the work laid down,
And joy that they have gained the victor's crown.

We call them dead—may we not rather say
   The living ones. For in the upper skies
They hold, with us, high festival to-day;
   They seek our own, those shining spirit eyes,
And mingling with our song their triumph tone,
They blend the joy of heaven and earth in one!

We may not see them with our earth-bound gaze,
   The music of their voices may not hear,
Yet from their presence come divinest rays,
   And to our inmost hearts we feel them near;
They bid us follow in the path they trod,
They lure us on to nobler work for God!

Oh, may the coming years a record be
   Of grander triumphs than the past hath won,
Oh, may the children, as the fathers, see
   An era of new miracles begun;
And, safe at last, may we together stand
A pilgrim host in God's own Promised Land!

The beautiful school room was made more attractive by reason of the flowers, banners and other decorations, tastefully arranged. On the platform were Rev. E. Evans, pastor of the church; the Rev. Henry Daniel, Messrs. Joseph Prichard, John Jackson, David Smiler, William C. Godsoe, Jas. Bustin, and representatives of other schools. It will be remembered that Mr. Bustin was a member of the first Sabbath school organized in St. John, the methods of which in teaching were in marked contrast with those of the present day. The first Sabbath school in Centenary was represented by Messrs. Jackson, Smiler, and Godsoe. The portrait of John Gardiner, the first superintendent, was placed in a prominent position, as was also the picture of "Centenary as it was."

The pastor of the church offered the opening prayer, and Rev. Mr. Daniel read the sixty-first chapter of Isaiah, after which Mr. J. McA. Hutchings gave an address describing the origin of the jubilee, making brief reference to his predecessors in the office of superintendent, and showing the condition of the school, which he considered flourishing. There were 428 scholars enrolled, and during the preceding year $653.14 had been raised; of that amount $384.34 went to the Missionary Society of the church. After describing the Missionary, Temperance, and Band of Mercy work, Mr. Hutchings said that former members of the school often proved their continued interest by gifts for the work. Among those friends was Mr. Edwin Frost, who had been very generous in his gifts, and had recently contributed $100 to the Library Fund.

Mr. Hutchings was followed by Mr. E. T. C. Knowles, who read an interesting paper bearing upon St. John Sabbath School history. Mr. Knowles had been a member of the infant, intermediate and bible classes, and, passing from a scholar, had been a teacher in the school for a number of years. While his address in some measure was in the nature of reminiscences, yet he also gave a brief sketch of the origin and progress of the Sabbath Schools in their bearing upon the celebration then being observed. The birthplace of the Sunday Schools in St. John has already received reference. The reader will remember that it was organized during the superintendence of Rev. William Black, in the summer of 1809, by George Taylor, an English school-master and Methodist local preacher. The schoool first met in the building then occupied by the Methodists as their place of worship, but known as the City Hall, afterwards for a time in the parsonage adjoining the new church, and then in the school building erected on Horsfield street, in the rear of the church.

In the year 1840, the year after the opening of the Centenary Church, then known as the new chapel on Great George street, the Germain street school was divided, part of it coming to the new church, and for a time holding sessions in its galleries. In 1840 the lady teachers, by a tea meeting, and through other efforts, raised £60, the beginning of a fund for excavating the rock under the church and constructing a school room. In the next year the scholars were able to meet in their own room. This room, like all basements, was unattractive. It was cellar-like, poorly lighted by low recessed windows, the floors and walls were often damp, and it was sadly void of beauty either of form or color. Evidently the school had earnest officers and teachers, for in the district minutes of 1841 we find the following report:

"St. George's Sabbath School.—The school in connection with this chapel is in a flourishing state. The labor expended has been owned of God in the conversion of some of the scholars. One has lately been transferred to the church triumphant. The school was formed in June, 1840, and now numbers 16 male and 15 female teachers, 92 male and 118 female scholars; total, 210; average attendance, 186. A library has been formed for teachers and another for scholars."

The report for 1842 is as follows:

"Centenary Chapel, Great George Street.—2 superintendents, 3 secretaries, 1 librarian, 18 male teachers, 20 female teachers—officers, 44; 166 male scholars, 177 female scholars—343; total, 387. School opened each Sabbath afternoon for two hours, commencing at 2 o'clock.

"Signed, JOHN GARDINER."

In 1852 there were 411 scholars; average attendance, 210. In 1853, 40 of the scholars joined the church.

At this time the school exercises had changed somewhat, the Bible and Catechism having superseded the arithmetic and writing book, but the primer lingered on in the junior classes until comparatively recent years.

In 1865, in the report made to district meeting, it was stated that during the year a number of scholars had been removed by death, but in every instance the death was hopeful and triumphant. Two teachers had exchanged mortality for life, one exclaiming. "Oh, who would not go to the Eden above!"

The above items, as will be observed, are selected at intervals. They fairly represent the reports which from year to year were submitted to the district meeting.

Superintendents.—The first superintendent, Mr. John Gardiner, held the office from the organization of the school until the year 1865. A quiet, earnest, steadfast Christian gentleman, he was loved by all connected with the school. In 1866, after his retiring from office, he was presented by the school with a portrait in oil of himself.

Mr. John Jenkins, for many years Mr. Gardiner's assistant, and then his successor, was a man of more rugged character, strong-willed, energetic, and alert for improvements.

Captain Joseph Prichard, who succeeded Mr. Jenkins, was a faithful and useful officer, and a great favorite with children. He reminded one of the parish priest in "Evangeline," of whom Longfellow says:

"And the children
Paused in their play to kiss the hand he extended to bless them."

SABBATH SCHOOL SUPERINTENDENTS.

JOHN JENKINS.   JOSEPH PRICHARD.
           JOHN GARDINER.
HENRY J. THORNE.   J. McA. HUTCHINGS.

Capt. Prichard was succeeded in 1880 by Mr. H. J. Thorne, who, during his term of office, was elected to the mayoralty of the city.

In 1886 Mr. John McA. Hutchings was appointed, and is still at the head of the school.

Some of the scholars have become Methodist ministers: Robert Duncan, Charles Dockrill, Arthur Whiteside, Edward D. Whiteside, Geo. Dixon, and Charles H. Manaton.

Before the fire of June, 1877, the school was in a prosperous condition, the average attendance being over 250. The fire was a great hindrance. The school lost its two valuable libraries, its records, and all its furniture, excepting the cabinet organ, a table, and the desk Bible, which had been presented by the late William J. Starr. On the 24th June, 1877, the Sunday after the fire, the attendance, when the school met in the galleries of the Exmouth Street Methodist Church, was only about thirty, and was not much over a hundred when, on the 18th November, 1878, the new and beautiful school building was first occupied. In 1882 the highest attendance was less than 200. In 1884 it had risen to 260, and in 1886, when Mr. H. J. Thorne retired from the superintendency, it had gone beyond 300; and has since then at times exceeded 350.

DEPARTMENTS.—*Missionary*—This work was begun by the institution of the Sabbath School Missionary Society, in March, 1865. The plan of working was to give the Sunday collections in the school and the collection at an annual meeting of the scholars to the mission cause. A few years afterwards it was deemed advisable to put this work in the hands of a committee, and, instead of the weekly collection, to take a special missionary collection on the first Sunday in each month. In 1885 the Christmas Missionary Thank-offering was instituted, and has been continued with good results. In this connection the name of Miss Hattie Smith (now Mrs. A. H. Eaton, of Baltimore, U. S.), is deserving of special mention.

Temperance.—In 1884 the temperance department was placed in the hands of a committee, under whose direction quarterly temperance meetings have been regularly held, at which, by addresses, object lessons, etc., the duty of total abstinence has been impressed on the scholars and visiting friends. The simple pledge—

> We do hereby pledge ourselves to abstain from the use of all intoxicating liquors as a beverage, and to discountenance their use in society—

has been signed by nearly all the officers and teachers.

Band of Mercy.—This branch of the Society for the Prevention of Cruelty to Animals has proved interesting to the scholars, and, under the care of Miss Mary B. Smith, has done good work. R. Ernest Smith, a member of the Centenary Band in 1888, was awarded the diploma for the best essay on Kindness to Animals, given by the S. P. C. A. of England, while in this, the second year in which competition has been held, Miss Edna Irvine, also one of Centenary's scholars, has achieved the same success. The two diplomas are placed upon the walls of the school room, and the school is justly proud of them.

The Library contains 900 volumes, well selected and in good condition.

Papers.—"Home and School," "Pleasant Hours," "Sunbeams," "The Missionary Outlook," and "The Sunday School Times" are taken.

At the present time it may be said that the school organization is effectively carried on,—the superintendent and his assistant being diligent in their offices, the teachers faithful in duty, and the scholars interested in the exercises.

At the Jubilee Services addresses were also delivered by Mr. W. J. Clark, of Carleton, representing the other Methodist Sunday Schools, and Mr. John Jackson, who was a scholar in the Centenary school at the time of its organization,

SABBATH EVENING SERVICE.

Long before the evening service commenced not a vacant seat was to be found in the body of the church, and when the opening hymn was announced the galleries were well filled. The meeting opened with the singing of the 28th hymn —

"God the Lord is King."

Prayer was offered by Rev. Howard Sprague, followed by the choir chanting the Te Deum.

The lessons were read by Rev. Dr. Pope from Isaiah, lxi., and Ephesians, ii. Between the lessons the choir chanted very sweetly

"Oh, sing unto the Lord a new song."

The sermon was delivered by Rev. Dr. Sprague, who took his text from Matthew, xiii., 31 and 33: "Another parable spake he unto them, saying, The Kingdom of Heaven is like to a grain of mustard seed, which a man took and sowed in his field. The Kingdom of Heaven is like unto leaven, which a woman took and hid in three measures of meal till the whole was leavened."

"The explanation of the utterance of this group of parables at that particular time is to be found, not in the natural scene, as has been sometimes suggested, but in the moral scene, hidden from others, but open to the eyes of the Lord. A careful study of the Scriptures proves that at this time the enthusiasm which attended Christ's Galilean ministry had reached its height. The crowd had gathered with great eagerness to hear what the Saviour had to say. The first two parables treat of the effect of Christ's ministry at that period, and describe the mood of the Saviour's mind, foreseeing that the majority of his hearers would either reject his message or accept it only in heartless assent or in a transient transport of enthusiasm. However, the pursuing excitement of the eager crowd did not deceive Christ. He told his disciples that they should not be discouraged or disheartened by lack of success in their ministry, and so gave them these two parables to teach them that his influence and kingdom would triumph over all hindrances.

"The two parables are very much alike and teach somewhat the same lesson. The mustard seed illustrates the growth of the Saviour's kingdom in the world. Both of them teach of its growth from a very small beginning, but the second differs from the first in that it explains the method by which the growth is to be attained. The first directs the thought to the growth of Christ's kingdom as a society or a church; the other leads persons to think of its secret, renewing power, gradually subduing all things to its influence. The mustard seed gives the fact that the kingdom grows from a small beginning to a great estate; the leaven teaches the law by which the progress is made, viz., the law of assimilation, and the use of the assimilated parts for further extension. The grain of mustard seed was relatively the smallest of all the seeds sown in the eastern countries, and very fitly shows how humble was the beginning of the Saviour's kingdom. He was born in a stable, clad in swaddling clothes, and laid in a manger, because there was no room for him or Mary, his mother, in the inn. The proof of his family's poverty is found in the fact that when, according to the Jewish law, the young mother went to present her child to the Lord and offer sacrifice, although his birth had been heralded by the angels, she was only able to present a very simple and inexpensive gift at the altar. Mary belonged to the line of David, and Jesus was his true successor, but the family had fallen into decay, and this was one of its poorest branches. He only appeared before the world for some thirty months, and his ministry only covered the narrow strip of country from Tyre to Jerusalem and from the Jordan to the sea. Added to this is the fact that Christ ended his ministry in apparent ignominy and defeat, deserted by his followers, and enduring death upon the cross. Therefore how fitly did Jesus take up the simile and say that the kingdom of heaven was like unto a grain of mustard seed.

"But a comparison of the beginning with the end makes the comparison all the more appropriate. Look at Christendom to-day. Through all the ages which have passed since Christ's time, it has steadily extended, and is still going forward with great force and swiftness. A rough estimate says that at the end of the first century there were but half a million Christians; in the fifth century 15 millions; in the fifteenth 100 millions, and now, at the end of this century, there are at the least calculation 300 millions who acknowledge Jesus as their Lord, Master, and Saviour. It is true that not all who count themselves Christians are such followers as Jesus himself would have acknowledged, for within the folds of Christendom, and amongst those who say its creeds, are to be found worldliness, sensuality and crime; but this glorious fact remains that his personal influence and invisible dominion is owned by people who, to-day, speak in 300 different languages, and are thrilled by the magic of his name. His influence and his power is felt even here and now, for he says: 'Lo, I am with you always, even unto the end of the world.' How has all this been wrought? Christ himself died 1800 years ago, but he has worked by means and methods. What have been the means and methods he employs? The second parable answers the question. Christianity gradually subdues and turns into Christ's own likeness whatever it comes into contact with. It communicates to the believer Christ's own nature, and is continually making fresh converts. It is true that Christ wrought his works in public and proclaimed his message on the mountain, by the sea, in the courts of the temple, and anywhere and everywhere that the people were wont to gather; but the nation, looking for the Messiah and the kingdom of God, saw no sign of its approach, and when it was set up in a few hearts and entering on its career of victory, did not know that it had come. But the leaven in the hearts of the few believers has made them so many centres of contagion. Paul and his fellow travellers went over the Ægean Sea and first spoke the name of Jesus on the European continent. They came to Phillipi, a city named after the great leader of the Macedonians. It was then a Roman colony, and soldiers of the empire occupied the fortresses on either hand, and their power then dominated the world. Upon that spot Paul laid the foundation of an empire which was destined to extend and go beyond the bounds of the Macedonian and Roman empires. How was it done? Upon the Sabbath day, according to his wont, Paul sought a place to preach the gospel to a congregation of Jews. He found there was no synagogue in the city, but supposed there was a place of meeting by the river side; so thither he went, and found a few women gathered together for worship. So few were present that it hardly seemed worth while to go through the formality of a public address, so he sat down and conversed with them about God, and told them the story of Jesus and his love. Its simplicity at once won a woman's heart, and in a short time not only she but her whole household confessed faith and were baptized in the name of the Lord. An Asiatic woman, a Greek slave, and a Roman officer were among the first members of the European Christian Church. In this way was laid the foundation and dominion of a church which has not only lasted in Europe to this day, but has extended its influence over the Atlantic and taken possession of this western continent. When one of England's most illustrious public men was asked, a few years ago, what he thought to be the most valid argument for the divine origin of the Christian religion, he said there were six, but the one which had the greatest influence with him was the successful propagation of Christianity, by moral means only, against the opposition of all the power, —physical, moral and intellectual—of the Roman empire, till finally it had triumphed over the empire itself. The success of a religion is no proof of its truth; but take all the circumstances into consideration, and in this case it is almost a demonstration. Nothing like it, except Mahomedanism, has ever swept over the world. But Christianity is unlike Mahomedanism, which put the nations to the sword and made conquest of them. Christianity, like the mustard seed, spread from heart to heart, town to town, until it had in every village, town or city, disciples who were ready to die in its defence.

"The parable teaches the importance of individual labor, of personal consecration to Christian work, and of the contact of man with man. The extension of Christ's kingdom depends upon the personal effort of each believer. It does not exist as an empire, but in the hearts of its believers. It is an invisible church. Christianity is not something in the air, to be breathed whether persons will or not, although in a sense even this is true. The spirit which Christianity brought into the world has so pervaded society and affected civilization that in its indirect benefits all must share. Even the most blatant infidel or atheist owes a thousand blessings to the religion he spurns and the Christ he contends against. Outside of this, though Christianity is a spiritual power, renewing men into the likeness of God, it is not an infection which men take they know not when or where, but it is a contagion which they get by contact with their fellows. Between the leaven and the meal there is a likeness and a difference; the difference makes the development of the process necessary, the likeness makes it possible. So there is a universal likeness in the spiritual nature of men, but between that nature in its ordinary developments, and that nature renewed and sanctified by the trust and spirit of Christ, there is a wide and eternal difference. The simple possession of that nature involves in all men possibilities high as heaven, glorious as the gospel, eternal as God. Therefore let us despair of none, however far they have wandered. They have still within them that which makes it possible that they will say, 'I will arise and go unto my Father.'

"During the fifty years that Centenary Church has been in existence the kingdom of Christ has been very widely extended. Since the apostolic age this century has been the most glorious in the history of Christianity. In the great movements of the last fifty years Centenary Church has done its share of the work. It may not have done all it could have done, but it has had a part in the glorious work, and may look back with thanksgiving to-day. It has had spiritual prosperity within the church itself, and the kingdom of Christ has always been present, sometimes in power. Many who have worshipped within its walls have gone to their final rest victorious over sin and death. The heart in the pulpit filled with the love of Christ has touched the hearts in the pews, and the hearts in the pews have, in turn, touched each other. The holy leaven has wrought its influence in the family circles and the groups of friends. This leaven has wrought from one generation to another. So may this leaven work great power during the coming years, until the Lord himself shall descend, and the dead in Christ arise, and 'they which are alive and remain shall be caught up together with them in the clouds to meet the Lord in the air; and so shall we ever be with the Lord.'"

At the conclusion of the sermon the choir sang as an offertory—
"Awake thou that sleepest."
Hymn 606—
"Come, let us join our friends above,"
was then sung, and the service closed with the benediction by Dr. Sprague.

The preachers of 1839 and the standard bearers of that time had now passed over to the great majority. A glance at the early rent roll will show that the depletion wrought by the ravages of time in the fifty years was most marked. The following is a list of the pewholders of 1839, inaccurate only, it is believed, in that, in a few instances, the names of some are found who really did not enroll themselves until the next year. It may be interesting to compare it with the list of those who were pewholders at the time of the jubilee :—

--- 1839 ---

John Knollin.
E. T. Knowles.
R. W. Thorne.*
James E. McDonald.
Thomas Gard.
George Dunbrack.
Samuel Coaks.
George F. Smith.
Isaac Johnston.
John Jones.
John Gardner.
William Whiteside.
George Thomas.
Thomas Nisbett.
Charles Crookshank.
William Wright.
Richard Whiteside.
George A. Lockhart.
William Brundage.
William H. Tyson.
Richard Riggs.
John Graham.
Nathan Clinton.

William Till.
John McAlpine.
Samuel Gardner.*
Richard Whiteside, Jr.
Nathan Godsoe.
John Stevens.
George Hardy.
Charles Thomas.
Aaron Eaton.
Henry Whiteside.
W. L. Brown.
William Curry.
Azor Betts.
Henry Campbell.
William Bean.
John Sharp.
Mary Payson.
William Salmon.
Edward Sancton.
John J. Munroe.*
Thomas P. Williams.
Thomas Leavitt.
Samuel C. Bugbee.

Samuel Bustin.
Jeremiah Gove.
Mark Varley.
William Nesbitt.
Reuben Watts.
Benjamin Underhill.
S. K. Laskey.
John McAuley.
W. H. Secord.
Edmund Davison.
Sweet and Robertson.
James D. Lewin.
Fields and Harrison.
Johnston Sullivan.
Christopher Noble.
Thomas Baldwin.
John Kirby.
William A. Robertson.
David Woodworth.
H. Harrison.
George G. Gilbert.
Travis, Bartlett and Hutchinson.

* These names, it will be seen, are the only ones which appear in the 1889 list.

AND HISTORY OF CENTENARY CHURCH.

---1889---

Andrew G. Gray.	Hon. Judge Palmer.	John Kain.
Mrs. William Sandall.	J. L. Thorne.	Miss Sharp.
Mrs. E. Ennis.	G. F. Calkin.	D. J. Brown.
J. S. Turner.	R. W. Thorne.	D. H. Hall.
C. J. Henderson.	Stephen J. King.	W. Kennedy.
Hon. Judge King.	L. H. Vaughan.	Mrs. James.
Miss Armstrong.	E. C. Elkin.	John Sealy.
D. J. McLaughlin, Jr.	George Nixon.	H. B. White.
George Jenkins.	Mrs. E. R. Moore.	Geo. A. Henderson.
Robert Law.	W. H. Purdy.	W. E. Earle.
Ward C. Pitfield.	W. H. Hayward.	Miss Thomas.
John H. Baird.	Hon. Judge Tuck.	C. D. Trueman.
John Mitchell.	T. D. Henderson.	R. C. Thorne.
Thomas Ellis.	Misses Smith.	P. W. Snider.
Rev. H. Pope, D. D.	S. D. Scott.	Capt. Babbitt.
Rev. H. Daniel.	J. J. Munroe.	LeBaron Robertson.
John E. Irvine.	James R. Ferguson.	J. U. Thomas.
Geo. H. Trueman.	Mrs. Piercey.	James Sullivan.
Mrs. Mary A. Mitchell.	J. Mowatt.	E. S. Hennigar.
Dawson McKendrick.	Richard Daley.	J. Wm. Roop.
Albert S. Hay.	Thomas Bustin.	R. Magee.
Alex. Lockhart.	A. T. Bustin.	John McPherson.
Frank E. Ketchum.	John A. Jones.	George Lynam.
G. R. J. Crawford, M. D.	Mrs. G. M. Barrett.	C. A. Gurney.
John A. Noble.	T. O. Sandall.	Wm. T. McLeod.
E. Le Roi Willis.	Fred. W. Dorman.	Miss Longley.
Mrs. Clara Dearborn.	James Dinsmore.	William Greig.
Frank G. Bent.	George Little.	William C. Jordan.
Mrs. W. H. Venning.	Miss Bookhout.	Frank Pitfield.
Lieut.-Col. A. Blaine.	F. E. Craibe.	C. D. Stewart.
Armstrong Elliott.	Miss Eaton.	F. L. Harrison.
John Jackson.	H. A. Austin.	F. S. Whittaker.
Walter Wilson.	I. C. Bowman.	Thomas Jenkins.
T. P. and J. A. S. Mott.	R. M. and W. G. Smith.	Hardress Clarke.
G. O. Bent.	C. A. Palmer.	R. W. McCarty.
J. Clawson.	Joseph Allison.	Wm. and J. W. Hazelhurst.
Mrs. Ilea.	S. Hayward.	J. H. Baisley.
E. T. C. Knowles.	John F. Bullock.	C. F. Robertson.
H. J. Thorne.	Thomas White.	A. C. A. Salter.
G. E. Fairweather.	A. A. Stockton, M. P. P.	Fred. W. Blizard.
H. A. McKeown, M. P. P.	J. E. Whittaker.	Thomas C. Hennigar.
J. Fletcher Dockrill.	T. Amos Godsoe.	R. Ward Thorne.
Mayor Lockhart.	Jos. Prichard.	Isaac G. Stevens.
W. Watson Allen.	J. McA. Hutchings.	Miss Sullivan.
James E. White.	T. A. Temple.	G. A. Horton.
Mrs. E. B. McLaughlin.	Rev. J. R. Narraway.	John Mullin.
Samuel Gardner.	Thomas Johnston.	E. W. Paul.
Mrs. J. V. Troop.	Matthew Paul.	Mrs. Andrew Lawson
Mrs. Kennay.	W. C. Godsoe.	H. G. Addy, M. D.
H. D. Troop.	Miss McCordock.	John S. Dunn.

MONDAY EVENING.

It was deemed proper that the first week evening should be set apart for glimpses at Methodism as it was and as it is— its progress, changes, and present polity. A. A. Stockton, Esq., LL. D., one of the trustees of the church, occupied the chair, and in his opening address contributed much to the historic interest of the occasion. He said the year 1839 was remarkable in the annals of New Brunswick Methodism, as in that year not only was Centenary opened, but Mr. Charles F. Allison first made his proposal to the Methodist authorities to set apart a very large portion of his fortune towards the organization of a Methodist College. Out of his generous offer grew the splendid college at Sackville. In the year 1839 the population of New Brunswick was 154,000, but during the fifty years it had increased to at least 350,000. The increase of Methodists in the province, though, was more than the natural increase of the population during that period.

Of Mr. Narraway's address on the constitutional changes of Methodism in Canada, Dr. Lathern, in the *Wesleyan*, wrote as follows :—

"An address by Rev. J. R. Narraway evinced many of the qualities which some of us remember so well as characteristic of his pulpit and platform efforts and oratory of other days. It was a genuine treat to renew one's impressions of logical sequence, raciness, splendid glow of style, the summer lightening gleams of wit or humor by which the subject was revealed, and to find that a voice which has been partially silenced for years has in some way recovered much of its former tone and clearness. It is more audible than at any period since retirement from full circuit and pulpit work. Mr. Narraway sketched rapidly the constitutional changes of Methodism in the Eastern Provinces during the past fifty years; the formation of the Conference of 1855, in affiliation with British Methodism ; the union of 1874, the formation of separate Conferences for each of the Eastern Provinces, and the organization of a quadrennial General Conference for Canada; the more recent union of all branches of Methodism in the Dominion, with a glance at its distinctive features. In all these changes, it was believed that on the whole there had been progress and increased efficiency. In giving impressions of several distinguished ministers of our church during the period under review a beautiful and discriminating tribute was paid to men whose names we shall not willingly let die. Some of them long ago rested from their labors, others more recently, but in all cases their lives exhaled so sweet a fragrance that the perfume lingers yet. We are solemnized by the thought of having been summoned to take an untarnished banner from hands stiffened in death, to be borne on to other successes. Because of such examples and such trust committed, have we not a higher character to sustain?"

Of Dr. Lathern's effective address on the progress of Methodism, it may be said that it abounded with interesting and suggestive statistics, and was replete with facts and information as to the wonderful growth of the Methodist Society from its inception to its 150th year. The hostility with which its doctrines were received, the obstacles with which it had to contend, and the success achieved, were admirably placed before his hearers, whom he exhorted ever to work with an eye single to the advancement of God's kingdom and the spread of Methodism.

TUESDAY EVENING.

Centenary has the unique distinction of numbering among its stated worshippers three of the six Judges of the Supreme Court of the province. One of these, Mr. Justice Tuck, a loyal adherent of the Methodist church, occupied the chair for the evening set apart for reminiscences. In talking of old times there would always be the danger of a speaker monopolizing time, while the idea of the committee for this meeting was that as many as possible should take part and that any person might feel free to do so. On account of the peculiar character of the meeting there was some foreboding as to its success. It was felt that it might be made interesting, and at the same time, for the reasons stated, there was the fear of failure. The felicitous address of the chairman, and the ease, dignity and grace with which that officer presided, relieved the uncertainty, and though the meeting was continued until a late hour, it was all too short.

J. W. Lawrence, Esq., was loudly applauded as he was introduced. Mr. Lawrence is a master in local historic lore, and delivered an excellent address. Methodist traditions, dates, and early development seemed as familiar to him as to the manor born.

Mr. James Sullivan, who had been a member of the Methodist Society from a period some years before the opening of Centenary Church, and a member of that church during all its fifty years, and at this date a local preacher, class leader, and probably the oldest official among Methodists in this city, being called on, furnished incidents and recollections of a most vivid and interesting character. These were particularly in reference to Messrs. Smallwood, Allison, Cooney and Albrighton.

It was expected that Senator Lewin would be present and speak of Rev. Enoch Wood and his pastorate, but he was not able to attend.

Rev. Henry Daniel, one of the early superintendents, and the oldest minister in connection with the N. B. and P. E. I. Conference, in the course of a most interesting address, referred in eulogistic terms to the labors of Rev. Enoch Wood and lay members Gilbert Ray, Thomas Hutchings, Aaron Eaton, George A. Lockhart, and others. Mr. Daniel's address was considered a marvel of intellectual vigor and sustained eloquence. It was not surprising that the learned chairman instituted comparison between the speech of the venerable minister and the prodigious efforts of Mr. Gladstone.

Mr. Justice Palmer was the last speaker, and as the earlier part of his life was spent in Westmorland, much of his address had reference to early incidents connected with Avard and others in their labors in that county. Judge Palmer had much to do with the building both of the school room and the church whose jubilee was being celebrated, and it was with knowledge of the facts that he awarded the crown of the present structure to the late accomplished Rev. Joseph Hart, and paid a graceful tribute to the intelligence, zeal and toil of that gentleman.

WEDNESDAY EVENING.

The Jubilee Love Feast was looked forward to with interest and is now cherished as perhaps the most pleasant recollection of the occasion.

From the files of the *Wesleyan* the following is taken:—

The Rev. Dr. Pope conducted a most blessed service, destined to be a cherished memory of the jubilee.

It was according to "the fitness of things" that the programme of Jubilee celebration should comprise a Love Feast service. One evening was set apart for that purpose. It was not like the Moravian Love Feast, held on the first day of the century commemorated by the church, at which the Wesleys received a baptism of the Holy Ghost for special work, continued until three o'clock in the morning. But like that of Fetter Lane it was "a pentecostal season indeed," and was with difficulty closed at a late hour; many feeling a sense of disappointment that there was not time for further testimony. The Centenary church was well filled on that occasion. No Methodist gathering in Halifax could show so large a number of venerable men, their hair once black as the raven's wing, now white as the snows of winter. Quite a number of them had been present at the dedication of the old Centenary church. More than one spoke of the "narrow stream," ready to say, "I pray, let me go over, and see that good land, that is beyond Jordan, that goodly mountain and Lebanon." Many a tribute was paid to departed worth. It was easy to realize in that hallowed hour that there were invisible spectators; encompassed about with a great cloud of witnesses. Never were the words of Wesley felt to be more apposite: "Even now by faith we join our hands with them that went before."

A report of this meeting was supplied to the *Wesleyan* by Mr. E. T. C. Knowles, and is as follows:

REV. DR. POPE expressed his regret at the absence of Rev. Fred'k Smallwood. The love feast is peculiarly appropriate to these jubilistic services, having been from the earliest days an institution of Methodism. The better part of our gathering to-night are invisible to us. They have crossed the flood. Let us summon up to mind the pious men of other days. I think to-night of the fathers of our ministry, many of whom I knew in my boyhood. We join hands with them, and, like the old Cornish Methodist, I would say, "Good luck to them in glory." We may be saved as they have been. As we commune with them the stream of death becomes a little brook. Soon we must cross over and join the majority. As I look at my venerable brethren, I feel that we, too, are to the margin come. This is my spiritual jubilee. In 1839 I passed from death to life. So I celebrate my jubilee with you. I thank God the same spiritual pulse of fifty years ago beats in my heart to-night. In my fellowship with you, both in the pastorate and as a member of this church, I have had many seasons of blessed communion whose memory I will always cherish. As I think of the blessed expectations, I feel like using the rude expression of the old Yorkshire Methodist woman, who, when dying, said : " He has promised to receive me to glory, and if he does he'll never hear the last of it."

DR. LATHERN — My experience is briefly stated in the words: "From sin and fear," etc. It is fitting that we should hold a jubilee love feast, as the memorable centenary year began with a love feast. Dr. Pope made the fire burn in my heart as he spoke of the past. I recall many of the honored men who labored here — those whose portraits look down on us, and others. Thomas Albrighton, whom I saw just before his death, having risen to distinction in the British conference ; William Wilson, an indefatigable toiler, who at the close of a Sabbath afternoon service, died in his carriage, and proved that sudden death was sudden glory; William Temple, of indomitable will and energy, whose mind wandered towards the close, but who, when called upon to pray, was at once recollected and exultant; William Smithson, whose latest theme was the great salvation, and whose latest utterance was the benediction at the evening prayer meeting - Arthur McNutt, who said, " Tell the brethren the gospel I preached so long sustains me now," and whose dying testimony was " Hallelujah, the star of Bethlehem shines brightly upon me;" the venerable Dr. Richey (I was with him in his last moments), recalled to his mind the phrase, " Resting on the infinite atonement of the Son of God," a wondrous light suffused his face. In the Government House, at Halifax, and over his mortal remains, the hymn was sung, "Come, let us join our friends above." I began my ministry in this country by preaching in the old Centenary on the morning of Christmas day, 1855, announcing a theme " God so loved the world," which since then has been growing on my sense of love and reverence. Appointed to St. John South Circuit after ordination in

1859, and to Centenary charge in 1868,—but dare not indulge in treasured reminiscences.

REV. WILLIAM LAWSON — Always ready to speak for himself and for his Saviour. Remember when I first landed here and preached for Bro. Lathern. The old Centenary bell had made me tremble, but God was with me and helped me. God is all in all to me and I to Him.

JAMES SULLIVAN — Glad to be where the Master is well spoken of. Was born again in 1830; became a leader in 1834; came in that year to St. John, and David Collins put me in his place in the class. God has always provided me a refuge from the storm. Seventeen years ago I was like to die, but a line or two said here to-night came to my mind, "From sin and fear and guilt and shame," etc., and I felt that God would raise me up again. Not where I ought to be, perhaps, but thankful for the cleansing blood, thankful for the prospect that I must soon cross the river. As the priests stood dry shod in Jordan, so our Great High Priest will bear us safely through the waters. May the Lord make use of us for His glory. Let us sustain our minister by faith and prayer, and God's blessing will be with us as in the past.

JOHN COLLINS — Seventy years ago my father took me, a little boy, to the love feast, and as I heard those whom I knew had been living bad lives were converted and serving God, I thought I wanted the same grace, and as I went out to care for the sheep, in my loneliness thought that God could save me — could save me now — could save me now for Jesus' sake. Then joy came to my heart and tongue, and my song was Glory to God. And I told them of it at home, and they rejoiced with me. Then the neighbors wanted me to pray with them, and God blessed me so that I formed seven classes. I was a baby then, and now, weak and infirm, but God can make children his strength. I have still the same Father to sustain me. Jesus' name saved me. We may go through services and ordinances, but without the name and spirit of Jesus to fill them, all is in vain. I hope God will revive his work here. Let us mind Wesley's rules and rejoice in Jesus as our friend and shield and comfort. May God bless you all. Mr. Collins sang "Saviour, let me walk with thee."

MR. DOUGLAS — Can see "Jesus only." Would glorify God. A stranger here to-night in the city of my birth, but I made a vow when I left my home in New York to glorify God, and want to do so now, for I have consecrated all to God. I see some here to-night who would know me, but very few. When five years old I became a scholar in the old Germain street Sunday school. I was converted here, and now I can say "my life is hid with Christ in God." He gives me the robe of his righteousness. It is fringed with 32,000 promises, and is dyed with the blood of Christ. Where I live we are not afraid to praise God.

GILBERT BENT — Thankful to be here. Many recollections of the past come up. How few of the young people of the old days reached full age! Recall many of the men of forty years ago, when 1 came here. They left a record that they now dwell in the house of many mansions, worshipping the Father above. But how few of those of forty years ago are here now! The message that comes to us is, "Be zealous and ready, for time flies by like the wind." As I think of the blessings and mercies of God, I feel that no one has so great cause for thankfulness as I.

REV. MR. MCLEOD — Glory to God! Jesus is my wisdom; in the knowledge of sin he is my righteousness and the knowledge of sins forgiven: he is my sanctification in the cleansing of my heart; he is my redemption, in that I hear him say "I have redeemed thee." Now there is nothing for me to glory in but the name of Jesus.

JOHN E. IRVINE—Looking over twenty-five years of Christian experience, I have a feeling of humility at the thought of how little I have done for my Master. God has blessed me during my short but precious association with this church. I think to-night that I ought to bear to the church the message given me a few months ago by the venerable Dr. McLeod, in Baltimore. He told of his visit to St. John after the great fire of 1877, and of his search for old friends. He could find only one, Mr. R. W. Thorne, but, said he, tell the friends at Centenary that I still pray for them. He gave me new encouragement, and should help us all to know that this venerable Christian, so far away from us, yet remembers and prays for us.

ALLAN KING—Glory to God! 'Tis a heaven below my Redeemer to know and to feel his blood flow. It is a blessed thing to know that Jesus is my friend. This is a glorious way to live. The dear Lord has done a wonderful work for me. He has sanctified every power of my mind and heart and will to his glory. I say "thank God for such a salvation."

TURNER HOWARD—I have been thinking the meeting is only for the old. When the Queen's jubilee came we heard a great deal of shouting, but we could not have that here, the church is so quiet. How glorious it is to be a Christian for fifty years, and then to preach for seventy-five years. I envy the fathers who have been long in the work. What a grand jubilee it will be when we get to the other shore; then we'll raise a shout. If I look to God here I will be glad in the endless jubilee of heaven. When we get there we won't look at the clock to see if it is near ten, but will be always praising our Redeemer. Glad I am a Methodist, for all I am I owe to them. Hope to live to be a hundred years old, that I may still be telling of the glory of this religion, which will last not for a jubilee time or for a century, but for eternity.

MRS. JOSEPH BULLOCK—I am glad I can praise God with one tongue. Have full salvation! Praise God for that. I have a jubilee of love and joy all the time. Like Father Collins, I am one of the Lord Jesus' little babes, to whom he had revealed things hidden from the wise. We are sugar and salt to preserve things. I rejoice that God preserves the simple. He keeps me sweet all the time. This is what full salvation does for me every day.

REV. EDWIN EVANS—One cold January morning, many years ago, in my own land, in a field, God took away the burden of my sins and gave me peace. The change was so great I felt as though I could fly, my soul was so full of joy. Praise God, this peace has lasted through all sorts of experience, and God is with me now. I know religion is true and is good, for all my experience through all these years convinces me of that. God gives me many glimpses of his love and power. He fulfils all his promises to the simple trusting soul.

MRS. D. J. MCLAUGHLIN—I have no doubt as to my conversion, and feel thankful for continued peace through simple faith in Jesus.

MRS. ELIZA ENNIS—I thank God I am a Christian and a Methodist. I am sure I love all Christians and churches, but especially this Centenary church. Forty years ago I gave my heart to God here, and I often think "I'd rather be a door keeper in the house of my God than to dwell in the tents of wickedness." The way is always growing brighter and better; Jesus is everything to me. To him I want to devote the best of my time.

Mrs. Baisley—Four or five years since God forgave me. Jesus is still precious to me.

James E. White—Not quite the jubilee of my conversion, but thirty-eight years ago I was aroused at a Baptist revival service. Can only sing "Once I was blind but now I see." Thirty years ago I came to this city an invalid. All the members of our class at Exmouth street—Dennis Sullivan, James Hale, David Collins, and others—are gone. How glad I am I took the stand I did! At a Baptist meeting, when the request for prayer was urged, I thought it foolishness, but afterwards, in a Methodist meeting, took the stand, and though people wondered at it, I have always been glad of it. My days here no doubt will soon be over, but I have confidence in God both for time and for eternity.

Rev. H. Daniel.—It was a pleasure to me to hear Dr. Lathern speak of the happy deaths of our ministers. As I look at the likenesses about us, they are nearly all men whom I knew. They died well. There are others whose portraits are not here—some who, at its beginning, were connected with this church, and who only recently have left us. I refer now to the late Edward T. Knowles, an active, devoted, spiritual man—devoted to his church. He was forward at all meetings for business or for religious purposes, and in his declining years, when his limbs trembled, and the tide of life flowed feebly, his word was ever "my hope is in God." I believe he died strong in the faith of the Lord, and is in the grand home of the Saviour. I have a blessed confidence in God. Have been nearly seventy years a member of the Methodist Church, or, as we used to call it, the Wesleyan Church. However, it is all one in Christ. Names matter little. The important thing is "Christ in us the hope of glory. God gave me a clear deliverance from sin. I have never had a doubt that my name was registered in the Book of Life. This has been my constant comfort even when Satan's buffetings were severest. The longer I live the more my faith is strengthened, and now my prayers have become rather praises and thanksgiving for the loving kindness, the boundless goodness of God. I feel it more than ever a duty to speak especially to our aged people as to their relation to God. The more so as they near the brink. Sometimes they have less confidence than we would wish, but to be able to speak a word of encouragement rejoices our heart. The love feast belongs to our people, and all who have come into the kingdom should feel free to speak of what God has done for them.

Mr. White—Not satisfied to leave without speaking for God. A stranger, but glad to share in witnessing to the goodness of God.

Joshua S. Turner—Fifty years ago next November God spoke peace to my soul. I was alone when the message came. Bless his name, he has kept me ever since, sometimes in a dark way, but he has never left me to myself. Sustaining and encouraging me by his smile and love, he is making my last days my best days. I remember, when I lived in Fredericton, Asa White, who always bore good witness. Glad to hear his brother, who has just spoken. Thank God for his sons and daughters who have grown up in this and other churches.

John McA. Hutchings—Glad I love the Lord Jesus. This is my daily joy. I find his service increasingly blessed and delightful. Happier now than when I began; my experience is one of increasing joy and peace and rest. My pleasure is in this service. My prayer and hope is that I may meet those who have gone before.

Mrs. Lemon (an aged lady)—My hope and confidence are in God. My old friends are gone and many of my dear ones are in heaven. I am waiting until called to meet them.

HENRY MAXWELL.—"There is a wideness in God's mercy like the wideness of the sea." These words came to my mind as I knelt here at the beginning of the service, and thought of the day more than fifty years ago, when I heard Dr. Wood preach on the foundation of the old Centenary Church. It humbles me in the dust to think of God's care for me. I stood at the death bed of Rev. Sampson Busby. It was a happy death. O that I may die the death of Sampson Busby. I praise God I have a hope of that.

REV. H. DANIEL — It was mine to bury Sampson Busby, and I have no doubt of his blessed transit from earth to heaven. Our people die well. It is a blessed thing to have such memories.

The meeting closed with singing of hymn "Our souls are in His mighty hand."

THURSDAY EVENING.

The reunion and musical exercises in connection therewith had been looked forward to with interest, were heartily entered upon, and much enjoyed. At eight o'clock all the seats in the auditorium were occupied by a congregation gathered to listen to the Jubilee Concert of Sacred Song. This meeting, as were all the others of the occasion, was opened with devotional exercises. It could not be expected that the first choir would be represented among the singers on this occasion, nor was it; but from 1849 down to the present time there were representatives. Those present were Mrs. Tuck, Mrs. Whittaker, Mrs. Brown, Miss McKillopp, Mayor Lockhart, and A. T. Bustin, of former choirs; and of the present, Miss Barnes, Mrs. H. J. Thorne, Miss McKeown, Miss Henderson, Miss Maud Godsoe, Miss Carrie Ellis, Miss Hattie Prichard, Miss Alice Hea, Miss Minnie Hea, Miss Annie Turner, Dr. Daniel (leader), Messrs. J. Clawson, W. A. Kain, Samuel Smith, and Henry Turner. Here and there in the audience, among the elderly people, could be noticed some who were members of the choir when the church was first opened. The first number on the programme was the grand old Easter anthem, sung so heartily as to bring vividly to mind the Easter exercises of other days. This was a time-honored anthem in the old church, and always rendered with so much strength of expression and musical effect as to make it exceedingly popular with the people.

Later on the anthems "I will Love Thee, O Lord" and "Arise, O Lord" were well rendered by the full choir. Of the soloists, Miss Barnes sang "Our King" with much expression and tenderness of feeling; Miss Alice Hea sang very sweetly and in a clear voice "The Lord will Remember His Children"; Miss Bessie McKeown's solo, "Heavenly Father," was beautifully rendered.

At nine o'clock an adjournment was had to the school room, where refreshments were served, and an hour was spent in conversation and sociability, occasionally broken by choice vocal selections by the young ladies of the congregation known as the "Treble Clef." Altogether it was felt that the programme was well conceived and happily carried out.

FRIDAY EVENING.

The chair was taken by His Worship Mayor Lockhart, and at the hour of opening, the church was nearly filled with an audience brought together by the announcement that an historical sketch would be read and the tablet unveiled. Reference in these pages has been made to Mayor Thorne. He was succeeded by George A. Barker, Esq., who died after having served but a few weeks. To the position thus made vacant W. A. Lockhart, Esq., was elected, and held office at the time of which we write. Mr. Lockhart had long been connected with the Centenary Church, and for a number of years his powerful voice greatly enriched the singing in the public services. Upon taking the chair, His Worship announced the object of the meeting, and gave the audience some interesting personal recollections in connection with the church's history.

G. A. Henderson, the trustee steward, was then called upon to read the historical sketch prepared for the occasion. His paper might be considered an outline of what has been presented in the foregoing pages. The term "outline" is used rather than "synopsis" or "abstract," as the matter which is here presented had not then been written.

Dealing with the financial feature, he showed the cost of the first church, which has already been stated, and of the new property.

The School Room cost		$26,173 96
New Church		53,437 80
Total cost present structure		$79,611 76
The insurance applied to the new building was about	$15,183 00	
Rec'd from Church Relief Fund	9,286 00	
" " Varley Trust "	7,700 00	
Contrib'd by congregation, etc.,	19,142 76	$51,311 76
Present indebtedness		$28,300 00
From the opening of the church in 1839, the amount contributed from pew rents is		$50,010 00
Weekly collections		77,537 00
Special efforts in paying debt of old church		26,000 00
Paid on new church by this congregation		19,042 00
To which must be added for missions and other church funds (probably more but say)		30,000 00
		$202,589 00

Trustees' current liabilities :—

*1843.			1889.	
Interest	£218	1,7	Interest	$1668 00
Sexton	25	0 0	Sexton	250 00
Candles and oil	17	0 0	Gas	300 00
Coal and wood	12	10 0	Fuel	320 00
Insurance	50	0 0	Insurance	125 00
Incidentals	10	0 0	Choir expenses	686 00
			Water rates	100 00
	£332	11/7	Ground rent	20 00
			Repairs to organ and building	125 00
			Incidentals	80 00
				$3674 00

* 1843 is selected as a fair year for comparison as church organization was then well effected and the congregations are said to have been large.

Pew rent receipts — 1843.................... $ 400 00
"   "   — 1889.................... 1900 00

Towards the choir fund special subscriptions, amounting to about $400, are annually made by members of the congregation.

This leaves to be provided for................... $3274
Receipts from pew rents............. $1900
From 5-year q'rt'ly-paym't subscriptions, 874
Quarterly Board appropriations........ 500 3274

In what has been said it is clear that our fathers were generous in their contributions, but it is not a fact that the present congregation is less liberal. During the last twelve years the contributions have been more than double those of the previous twelve years.

To the Mite Society, at that time under the presidency of Miss Bartlett, and with Miss Palmer as treasurer, was accorded praise for the help extended by it to the church in its financial relations. The other agencies which had been so effective in their contributions to the funds of the church received mention, and, though the time was limited, the speaker sought to place before the audience the leading features of the fifty years in their relation to the church, its organization, development, present position, and outlook.

As the sketch was finished the officials of the church gathered around the communion rail with a view to the unveiling of the tablet, in the active part of which the trustees were represented by their oldest member, Mr. Richard W. Thorne, while Mr. James Sullivan, the senior member of the Quarterly Board, represented that body. Mr. Thorne, in making the presentation, read the following:

In the name of the Trustee and Quarterly Boards of this Centenary Church, we present this Tablet in commemoration of its Jubilee and in grateful memory of the Pastors who have labored among us during the past fifty years. RICHARD W. THORNE,
On behalf of the Trustees.
JAS. SULLIVAN,
On behalf of the Quarterly Board.

As the reading was concluded, Mr. Sullivan caused the Union Jack, which had covered the tablet, to be removed. The tablet was made by R. H. Green, and reflects credit on his taste and skill. It is shield-shaped, made of brass, mounted on walnut, and engraved with letters of red and black, and bears the following inscription:

THIS TABLET
was erected

ON THE OCCASION OF THE

Jubilee Celebration,

IN GRATEFUL RECOGNITION OF FAITHFUL SERVICES

OF THE  WHO FOR

FIFTY YEARS HAVE MINISTERED TO THIS

Congregation.

—◆✠◆—

CHURCH DEDICATED, AUGUST 18, 1839.
DESTROYED BY FIRE, JUNE 20, 1877.
SABBATH SCHOOL ROOM OPENED, NOV. 17, 1878.
SECOND CHURCH DEDICATION, AUGUST 27, 1882.

Rev. Mr. Evans and Dr. Pope suitably acknowledged the gift.

Miss Sarah E. Smith then read her beautiful Jubilee poem, which has already received a place on these pages among the Sabbath school exercises. Judge Palmer and Judge Tuck delivered short addresses, and the exercises were closed by the singing of the Doxology.

SUNDAY, 25TH AUGUST.

With the unveiling of the tablet it had been intended to bring the Jubilee services to a close, but just as the programme had been completed the pleasing intimation came that the services of Rev. John P. Newman, D. D., Bishop of the M. E. Church of the United States, could be had for Sunday, 25th August. Efforts had previously been made to secure Bishop Newman's presence, but it was supposed without success. He was, however, able to so arrange his plans as to be in St. John on the day named, and occupied the pulpit in the morning and evening. Great congregations gathered to hear the distinguished divine, whose fame as an eloquent pulpit orator was not confined to the country or continent in which he lived, or to the denomination with which he was connected. They expected to listen to discourses original in conception and brilliant in style. Their highest wish was gratified by the powerful and beautiful expression of the truth as it fell from the lips of the eloquent preacher. His theme in the morning was "Consecrated Individuality," based on John xi., 28: "The Master is come and calleth for thee"; and in the evening he discoursed on "The Great Conversion," his text being Acts xxvi., part of the 14th verse: "Saul, Saul, why persecutest thou me?"

Mrs. Newman, who accompanied her husband, addressed the Sabbath school in the afternoon, and on Monday afternoon she spoke on Missions before the ladies of the Methodist Missionary Society.

On Monday evening a large and representative audience assembled in the church and listened with great delight to Bishop Newman in his lecture on "The March of Civilization." Upon this occasion His Honor Judge King presided.

With Monday evening the Jubilee exercises closed. The design of the meetings was to appropriately observe the interesting period reached in the history of the church. That due recognition was given to that event will be admitted. There was no determined effort to make it an occasion for raising money, though collections were made at each service, and an opportunity given to the friends to make a free-will offering on Friday night. As a result of the contributions the sum of $628.45 was placed to the credit of the church.

A prominent church is an important factor in moulding the life of a community—how important no one can tell. Such for fifty years Centenary has been. It has stamped its influence on the life of Saint John. In a restless world change is always taking place. It is written on the community, on the congregation, on the home circle. During the fifty years multitudes have gone from within the walls of our church and are to be found in all parts of the world, perhaps actuated by the impulses which were formed in the old church home. If so actuated, it is evident that the influence of a church is outreaching to an extent altogether unappreciable, and is not confined to the city within whose bounds it is located.

The history of Centenary Church can never be written in full. The spiritual struggles, the triumphs of faith, the exerted influence, would be interesting indeed, but will only be known in that day when the hidden things shall be revealed.

Time, the waster, has rubbed most of the names from the list of fifty years ago. The youth have grown old—the old have passed away. Depletion has alternated with impletion. The workmen have been buried, but the work has been carried on. The services are now conducted by ministers, and the affairs of the church administered by officers who, for the most part, fifty years ago, had not been born. "We spend our years as a tale that is told," yet "we consider the days of old and the years that are past." We raise our "Ebenezer," and inscribe "Hitherto hath the Lord helped us." Our prayer for the future is, "Peace be within thy walls."

       We thank Him for the era done,

       And trust Him for the opening one.

www.ingramcontent.com/pod-product-compliance
Lightning Source LLC
Chambersburg PA
CBHW032145160426
43197CB00008B/780